CHISELED
BY
TRIAL
SCULPTED BY GOD

Gardiner B. Jones III, M.S.S.

Φπ
Phronesis Publishing

Chiseled by Trial: Sculpted by God

ISBN: 978-0-578-05367-7

Published by:

Phronesis Publishing
PO Box 433
Nolensville, TN 37135
http://www.chiseledbytrial.com

Printed and bound in the United States of America.

Cover design by Michael G. Jones
Cover photo by David Hancock
Author photo by Lisa K. Jones

DEDICATION

This book is dedicated to all those who suffer and wonder how a loving God could allow such things to happen.

ACKNOWLEDGEMENTS

I am pleased to acknowledge and thank my Lord and Savior, Jesus Christ, who continues to shape me with hammer and chisel. That is a good thing! Thanks also to the Holy Spirit for inspiring me to write this book.

How can I adequately thank my wife, Carol, who ignited the spark for this book? I deeply appreciate the many hours of sacrifice she made in allowing me to sit and write. I owe her so much more than I could ever repay.

I offer my humble gratitude to my brothers and sisters in the Lord at Franklin Vineyard Church: Pastor Jon Sterns who restored my trust in church leaders, and in particular to the Stephens Life Group—Dave & Susan Schuster, Debra Nunziato, Deborah & James Mohline, and Tony & Renee Lomelino. These wonderful people encouraged me and spent hours reading and discussing the material in this book, offering excellent suggestions.

My heart-felt thanks to Tim and Cherish Cart of Strongtower Media Services LLC for spending months editing this book and making invaluably constructive recommendations. You are truly wonderful people.

My firstborn, Michael Jones, I cannot begin to express what a fantastic job you did with the cover design. God has bestowed tremendous artistic talent on you. Thank you also to David Hancock for the cover photo that is so full of action.

To all my children, Michael, Matthew, Lisa and Tiffany, thank you for enduring me during some of the worst of my trials.

A special thank you to David "Skip" Prichard of Ingram Content Group, who was gracious enough not only to read the manuscript of an unknown author, but who believed in me, encouraged me and helped in getting this book into print. Thanks also to Lighting Source and Ingram Content Group because without them this book would still be just a file on my computer.

Finally, thank you to all who influenced my theology and fed my hunger to learn, particularly my mentors: Drs. Ronald E. Cottle, Ian A. H. Bond, Bobby Howard, Susan Keith, Mike Mansfield, Robert Gaulden, Mike Chapman, Ken Sumrall, Judson Cornwall, Fuchsia Pickett, Peter Wagner and Stephen Mansfield; Revs. Terry Mahan, Gary Beasley and Ken Gaub. The lessons they taught me were not only theologically deep and wide, but also filled with practical wisdom.

TABLE OF CONTENTS

PROLOGUE

When swelling and pride come, then emptiness and shame come also, but with the humble (those who are lowly, who have been pruned or chiseled by trial and renounce self) are skillful and godly wisdom and soundness.[1]

Proverbs 11:2

This book is intentionally personal because the trials we go through in life are intensely personal. I do not intend it to be clinical. My purpose is to share with you some stories and the lessons learned from the painful places through which I have walked, and often only crawled: divorce, death, murder, layoffs, financial ruin, broken trusts, a church that emotionally and spiritually killed their wounded, even my own pride and stupidity which have caused me to stumble and fall many times. The list is long. They are, more importantly, the places where God has spoken into my heart, teaching me to hear his intimate whisperings, bringing change and correction, teaching and rebuke; and where he continues to chisel me into the man he desires me to be. It is about how God has molded and sculpted me, bringing me low in order to fill me with wisdom and healing. It is my prayer that, because we all go through hard times, what I have learned in those places may help you in yours.

Contrary to the old childhood line, "Sticks and stones can break my bones, but words will never hurt me," we know that words *can* hurt, and God's words are no exception. The difference, though, is that when his words—and what he allows in our lives—cut, it is in order to shape us into who we need to be for *his* glory.

There is an old line in the fitness arena, "No pain: no gain." The same is true for the formation of our character. If we do not persevere through our trials, experiencing the pain, then there is no gain for us.

What follows in this book are not fluffy-cloud abstract ideas. They are a combination of biblical wisdom and down to earth, nitty-gritty truths born out of the painful places of life. You will certainly find some theology here; however, the main purpose of this book is to share with you how God has taken up his hammer and chisel and, despite my own pride and efforts sculpted me into a wiser person who is able to bring him joy. It is the story of my walk through the trials of life into healing and acceptance of his plans for me, and it is my hope that these lessons will speak to you when you are in hard times.

His words in times of trial are as real to me as the sound of my heart and more personal than the words of love I share with my wife. More significantly, they have taught me how much he cares about us and how he longs to be involved in our lives.

He isn't a God who created everything and then left it to run its own course. Our world is not on autopilot and is most assuredly not accidental. God cares. He's in our midst, and he wants to be there, close to us. One of the most amazing aspects of God is that despite his ability to be everywhere—and that means not just spread really thin, but all of him everywhere all at the same time—he desires to be intimately involved in my life, in your life.

So, who wants to be tested or sculpted by God's hammer and chisel? I do, and no, I am not crazy. I don't want pain or suffering anymore than do you, but God has gone through every trial *with* me. Each time he has chipped away more of what holds me back from a closer relationship with him, and I'm certain more is in store for me. That's what the difficult places of life are all about: stretching, teaching, learning, sculpting and molding us.

The apostle James commanded us to rejoice when trials come at us. At first that sounds strange. I mean, seriously, who gets excited about hardships? We can, however, learn that trials help us to build endurance, consistency and patience.[2] On the other hand, if you're like me at all, then just thinking about hard times can make you want to lock yourself away from God.

Over the course of many years I have learned to value the trials of life because it is there that God shapes our true character.[3] It is there that God has been closest to me, and it is there that you will find him closest to you. The daunting challenge for me has been to share the private places where God whispered into the deep recesses of my heart, where he has struck hardest with hammer and chisel. The prospect of describing the spiritual lessons learned in these places was nothing short of intimidating—which may explain why it took me so many years to begin. It was particularly difficult because in some cases I still feel the sting of some of the heartaches and trials through which I have come. It was also a time for me of healing.

When I was eight years old, my mother gave me my first copy of the New Testament. Fifty years later I still have it. The small book with its illustrated cover has remained a treasure to me, and even though the King James English was unnatural to my childish ear, God spoke to me from it. I loved reading the Sermon on the Mount and the Beatitudes. Their poetry touched something in me, and even in their simplicity I knew there was more meaning buried there in the words of Jesus than first met the eye. I realized they were the recordings of what Jesus had to say about life and God's kingdom. It wasn't until I was an adult that I would develop a much deeper understanding of his words.

Matthew's recording of The Sermon on the Mount begins with the phrase "And he opened his mouth and taught them saying …"[4] In the ancient Greek in which this gospel was written, Matthew begins with what is both a preface to a life-changing statement and one which means "to come over and whisper." That really struck a chord in me. Christ's teaching was less of what we have traditionally thought of as a sermon and more of an intimate conversation between dear friends—the Savior-Redeemer speaking gently and lovingly with those for whom he so deeply cares. You can almost sense his passion as he leans close to your ear to whisper his words of love.

God most often speaks this way to me. When I quietly lay my head against his chest, when I cast off all my worries and allow my mind and my heart to focus on him and him alone, then he speaks softly to me as the lover of my soul. These conversations not only blessed me, they are what kept me going even when I thought I could go no further. It is my prayer that you will discover him there too. Like a runner, they became what motivated me to keep plodding onward.

In late 1979 I ran my first marathon (26 miles). I had trained for a year. For the last three months before the race I ran every day and was running 60 miles a week. Each Saturday I ran a 20-mile course out through the over 100 degrees heat of parched pear orchards in Solano County, California, and then later along the salt-air and deep blue ocean shores of Diamond Head in Hawaii. Now 20 miles may sound like a lot, but let me assure you there's a big difference between running 20 miles and running 26 miles.

The day of the race finally arrived. Anticipation, wonder, fear and excitement were all tied up together inside me. It seemed surrealistic in the pre-dawn darkness of Honolulu that morning, standing with thousands of others by Honolulu Harbor. The strange mix of pre-dawn dark, the almost alien ozone orange of the streetlights combined with the cacophony of 10,000 runners made it all feel like a dream.

For blocks we gathered in a mob of silent frenzy. Then the gun went off! The mass—a huge herd of detached runners who had somehow become no longer strangers but family—began to move, slowly at first, then gained momentum until in a short while we were strung out for miles. And, oh! You should have seen the crowds! By the tens of thousands they lined the course, shouting words of encouragement, clapping and cheering each runner on, handing us cups of water and gloriously delighting in our efforts. The atmosphere was electric!

The onlookers so energized me that, without realizing it, I began running faster than that for which I had trained. It wasn't long before the damage was done. Something at the back of one knee tore. The race became very painful and far more of an endurance test than I could have imagined. A little while later, because of the pain, I stopped running and began to walk. As I walked, my knee began to lock up, so I started again slowly to jog. A few minutes later the pain once more forced me to stop and limp along. As my knee began to stiffen up yet again, I forced myself to resume jogging, only to quickly repeat this cycle of stopping, walking and jogging. It struck me that if I stopped again I wouldn't finish the race. That thought alone tore at me more than the searing pain in my knee. I had trained so hard and come so far. I just couldn't let it end there on the side of the road, so I forced myself to continue the last twenty miles in pain.

From that ordeal, I learned a valuable lesson not only about myself but also about this thing we call life: even when we are literally or figuratively in great pain we can go farther than we think we can. From a literal perspective in the marathon, it became a matter of continuing to put one foot in front of the other. Figuratively speaking, in whatever difficult place you are in—be it physical, emotional, spiritual, relational, financial and so on—if you will keep putting one foot in front of the other you too can make it.

For the record, I finished the race, sprinting the last quarter mile. I made it to the end not merely because I had trained hard for it, but because I chose to endure the pain in order to achieve the goal of finishing the race. You can reach your finish line too if you will—with God beside you—endure your pain and press onward.

While I hope to give you something to reflect upon, my deeper desire is to touch your heart. It is because I know God cares about these matters and each of us that I am willing to write of such personal issues and events. My prayer is that through this book God will speak to you in some way that helps you to accept his sculpting and that will help you through your trials.

Chiseled by Trial

DEALING WITH DEATH

Any man who doesn't cry scares me a little bit.

H. Norman Schwarzkopf,
Retired United States Army General, commander of
CENTCOM during the Gulf War and affectionately known as
"Stormin' Norman"

The subject of death is a difficult one for just about all of us, and yet it is something we all must face.[1] There's no getting around it: if not the death of someone we love, then eventually we will have to deal with our own death. We all fall into one of two camps: we either have never had to deal with death, and therefore cannot understand it even if we think we can, or else we have had to face the death of someone near and dear to us. My heart goes out to those who are in the midst of dealing with death or an impending death. I've been in those shoes far too many times already.

There's not much you can say that will help a person who has just lost, or is about to lose someone they love so don't speak up just to say something. The Bible doesn't instruct us to come up with some sort of feel-good story to try to lift another's spirit. Instead, it gives us solid, down-to-earth advice. It tells us to weep with those who weep.[2]

Cry with them. Share in their grief. Life isn't fair. It often hurts more than we can bear, and because of that we need each other more than some of us are willing to admit. If you really care about how someone else feels—or if you're in the place of having to deal with the death of someone you love—begin by understanding that grieving is normal.

The desire to hide from grief and pain is just as normal. Even Jesus, twice in the same night in the Garden of Gethsemane, recoiled from what lay before him when he asked God to take away what he knew was coming: separation and death.

This inclination to pull away from what hurts us is as natural a reaction as pulling your hand away from a hot flame. Don't feel either you must be a pillar of strength or as cold as ice. Death hurts, but if you know Jesus then the pain no longer has the upper hand. The good news is Jesus overcame death once and for all; and "once and for all" means more than just "forever." It also means "once and for everyone."[3] Even though we still have to face death, and it hurts in nearly indescribable ways, it is not the end of everything we hold dear. It may feel like it so to us at the time, but dear ones know that life goes on and so must you.

By all means, in realistic and practical ways do what you can to comfort those who are mourning, but at the same time be honest with them. It means far more to bring supper to a grieving family, or to truthfully say, "I can't even begin to understand how you must feel," and to then cry with them—feeling and sharing their grief with them—than it does to say something meaningless in order to just say something because you feel uncomfortable. We don't like sharing others' hurts, yet we often find that we need to have others share in our pain, don't we? Understand that words are not always necessary, and sometimes they just get in the way. More often in times of deep sorrow a good long hug, a shoulder to cry on or just being there says more and is more of a real help than anything we could possibly say.

I still remember the devastation of a teenage girl a few years ago. She was legally blind, and up to that time her only boyfriend, her total support system was her gallant Wesley. He died with his grandparents in a horrible car accident. I wrote a short article for our church newsletter about Wesley and his death. I didn't sugarcoat it, and I didn't try to make it sound as if everything was okay. I simply expressed as best I could how his death grieved me as well, and how I empathized with her in the sadness of her loss. A short time later, while still in the throes of grief, she gave me one of the biggest hugs I have ever had and thanked me for being real.

My honesty meant more to her than all the words of assurance many had been offering that, "in time everything will be alright." Let's be honest: sometimes everything doesn't get fixed. Comfort more often comes in our being honest and showing true compassion; and that simply means not playing games about the pain of death with those who grieve. Hurt with them. That helps more than we think it does.

Writing of Jesus, the prophet Isaiah said that "He was despised and rejected and forsaken by men, a Man of sorrows and pains, and acquainted with grief and sickness…"[4] He spoke of Jesus as one who knows firsthand what it's like to be sick, anxious, afflicted, the victim of varying evils and calamities. Speaking of Jesus, the New Testament writer of the book of Hebrews said that because of his suffering and testing Jesus is able to quickly come to those who are being tested and tried—those who are being exposed to suffering.[5]

The word used in Hebrews there is the ancient Greek word that means having been put to the test, having been tried or having experienced.[6] So then, in the context of dealing with death, it means that Jesus has shared the same experiences and the same trials that we go through so that he is able to comfort and console us.

When I feel grief, that's the exactly the kind of person I want around me—someone who understands how I feel because he's been there and has felt the same kind of pain. Jesus does understand my hurts. As a man, he was hurt. He knows all too well how that feels. He knows firsthand what rejection feels like, how painful it is when a close friend dies; the frustration, loneliness and even anger one feels when people misunderstand you; the anger, bitterness and frustration that accompanies unjust accusations, the pain of physical brutality and murder.

I am not interested in a god who is not connected with his creation, who cannot fully understand my concerns, desires and heartaches. The God I serve does indeed understand better than any of us the pain and grief of death.

What I am about to share are some of my experiences with the deaths of people I loved dearly, of what God spoke into my heart through each of those trials, and how he used his chisel to shape me in them. If you are experiencing the loss of someone you love, I pray that these stories will speak to your heart and help to meet the need you have for compassion and an understanding of your pain.

My Mother's Death

When I moved from Honolulu to New England at the end of the summer of 1983, my mother had just been diagnosed with cancer and probably weighed close to 200 pounds. She surgically lost her pancreas and half of her stomach and intestines. During this time, my wife drove her to chemotherapy for months while I was living 5,000 miles away instead of where I belonged.

In one of my worst failures, I broke both my vow to my wife and her trust by committing adultery, and then left her and our two sons. I broke her heart; and it was only God who sustained her for the year and a half that I turned my back on her, on our children and on our God. It was a crushing blow to her in many ways, but it also became a time for her of depending on God. As she put it to me later, during that time Jesus became her husband. I am amazed that God brought me forgiveness, and to us as a couple healing and restoration.

After my wife and our young sons rejoined me two years later, I looked on my mother again in that hospital room. She could not have weighed more than 70 pounds soaking wet. She looked like nothing more than a skeleton with skin. It was a very shocking and disturbing picture for me—one I will never forget. I have seen it since with others, and it is no less disturbing with each occurrence.

In July 1986 I was in the field on military maneuvers when the call came informing me that my mother was about to succumb to the cancer that had decimated her body for three years. I flew from New England to Honolulu as quickly as I could. She lived for about a day after I got there—in pain and unable to effectively communicate with anyone in her hospital room other than perhaps God.

Medical personnel said she was comatose, but it was obvious to all those present that she knew I had arrived. The moment I entered her room she tried to sit up. Even though she could not sit or speak, the moment I came into her room she tried to. It was as plain as day to all of us that she knew I was there. It was equally obvious that she was in tremendous pain.

Seeing her that way I prayed that I would never die in a like manner. I think I would rather be shot in the gut than to die the way she did: long, painfully, agonizingly slowly and yet so quickly to those of us who were healthy.

At one point as her body twisted in pain, I stepped into the hallway and asked a nurse to administer some more morphine to ease her pain. That she was showing any sign of pain was significant. You see, my mother had an extremely high tolerance for pain. She never allowed dentists to use Novocain or other painkillers. When it came to pain she could have made a U.S. Marine look like a sissy.

She took the pain, and went on without so as much as a whimper. What would make most of us scream never elicited any indication from her. So, for her to display any sign of pain meant that what she was feeling was far more than most of us could bear. The nurse refused, saying she did not want to make a drug addict of my mother. That angered me, and I think I had some unkind words for her. It was obvious to even a casual observer that there would be no addiction, only death and that in a short time.

As you can imagine, her death two days after her 64th birthday was painful for me. It was my first real encounter with the death of someone I loved. Three of my four grandparents had died earlier, but I had never been close to them, so my mother's death hit me quite hard. I cried for weeks and mourned for months. Coupled with the pain of loss was the knowledge that I had contributed to her emotional pain and that she had never heard an apology from my lips. Following on the heels of her divorce several years earlier, I knew my actions in leaving my wife had been yet another crushing disappointment to her.

And so I grieved, not only because she had died but also because she had departed this life without knowing that I deeply regretted the pain I had caused both to my wife and to her. As with her tolerance for physical pain, she had—without a word—taken the emotional pain of my failure and pressed on with life under an even heavier burden. I had made her life less bearable.

What did I learn from my mother's tortured death? What could God say to me to ease the pain of my broken heart? As simple as it sounds he said, "I love her too." It took a long while for me to grasp the full meaning of that. The God of all creation loves my mother more deeply than it will ever be possible for me to love her.

My mother had a hard life. As a child of The Great Depression, she learned early on—as are many now—what it means to go without. My mother and father struggled in their relationship for many years and when I was in my early twenties, it ended in divorce. She never recovered from that, but instead silently endured it as she did with all other pain.

Looking back I can see how the harshness of her life shaped her—making it hard for her to express her love, making her guarded about her deepest desires and longings, keeping her defenses up all the time. I loved her deeply, but God loves her even more. I do not say that merely because I want to believe it. God does love each of us more than we can ever fathom in this life. Need proof? He sent his Son to die for us when he could have just allowed us to reap the penalty of our own sin. He did not have to do that, but he loves us so much that it was what he wanted to do in order to buy us back and restore us to him.

From God's perspective, her death was not a horrible thing—although from our human point of view it was in both its coming and its going. It was, instead, a release for her. She no longer had to put up with the pain—emotional, mental and physical—that had haunted her life for so many years. Now she is with God—set free at last. She is in a place where there is no more pain, no more tears, no more being alone, no more lies, no more need. Of course I miss her, but I am also glad for her.

There is no way I could have understood that then because I had not yet gone through the places where God spoke into the depths of my heart, teaching and comforting me. Now I understand better. The experiential and spiritual "knowing" did not come quickly. It rarely ever does. God's lessons are more like crock-pot cooking—slow and consistent until, in the end, we're perfected through and through. More than twenty years later I still miss her, but she really is in a much better place and a far superior life, and that comforts me.

My Father's Death

My relationship with my father was quite strained for many years. Through my teens and into my thirties, he and I had difficulty being in the same room together. I frustrated him to no end, and he gave me plenty of reason to be frustrated as well. I mostly obeyed him because I knew the consequences of not doing so would be harsh. It was a quandary: I deeply desired and needed his respect (and did not receive it) and yet I was unwilling to live as he expected. Let us just say we did not enjoy one another's company very much. If he came into a room, I left, and vice-versa. It was uncomfortable for both of us.

Dad was a highly intelligent man, but if you did not know him well he came across as cold and uncaring. He had a razor sharp wit—an almost insane sense of humor. For example, a few months after Time magazine photos circulated around the world of the Vietnamese monk who set himself on fire in protest of the war, my father went to a costume party dressed as a Buddhist monk—complete with orange robe, skullcap and a gas can. He was passionate about the issues that concerned him, but failed miserably at showing affection and being unselfish with his children.

My impression of my father in those days was that he was a cold, hard, almost ruthless man who was so full of himself that he was unable to realize I was a rational though fallible human being who could hold an opposing yet intelligent viewpoint. He seemed to disapprove of everything I valued or believed in. None of my or my sibling's friends liked coming to our house. They were all intimidated by him.

He knew I had a good brain, and I think what infuriated him was seeing me not using it in the ways he thought I should. Granted, I made a lot of foolish choices early in life—ones I regret now. For example, he despised the fact that I had absolutely no interest in going to college after finishing high school. I really did not even care about finishing high school, much less of going to college. I wanted to become a Harley-Davidson mechanic, and one does not need a college education for that trade. To my dad that was an outrageously stupid mindset, and in retrospect it was indeed. He believed that kind of thinking was dooming me to a subservient life.

What probably bothered him the most was seeing in me all the same weaknesses and failures with which he had struggled. Having come to this realization I now understand myself better. In his own way my father was trying to keep me from making the same mistakes he had made. He did love me, but his methods—that generally consisted of coming down on me like a ton of bricks—only served to drive me further away. He cared, but did not know how to express it in ways I could understand then. Part of that failure was his, and part of it was mine.

Throughout high school and the years immediately following, the war in Vietnam raged. Coming from a long line of patriots and a proud military family history, my father despised my reluctance to serve in the armed forces during the war. He thought I was being a coward. I did wind up in the Air Force in 1972, near the end of the war, and perhaps that is what redeemed me in his mind for a season. I stayed in the military until 1995. Surprisingly what had to me seemed the worst possible thing to do turned out to be one of the best. Anyway, I think he expected me to run right out and enlist in the army.

I agonized over what to do. As a teenager in the 60s, I was strongly opposed to the war—as were most of my peers—but also knew I could not apply for conscientious objector status because if anyone in my family was attacked I would do everything within my power to defend them. I knew that if someone I loved was in deadly peril, without hesitation I would use deadly force to defend him or her.

When I got married at the age of 21 my father was so strongly opposed to my doing so that he refused to come to the wedding. Just as when I had no desire to go to college, he again believed I was making the most monumental mistake of my life. He would save me from my stupidity by not budging. If not for the threats of my mother, he would not have attended. Ultimately, he attended but sat defiantly through the ceremony with arms folded across his chest and his chin thrust out as if to say, "I may be here against my will, but you are still an idiot."

Having painted a rather unfavorable picture of him, I would like to take a moment to say that despite my rebellion and frequent dislike of him, I deeply respected my father. We did not often get along well, and it was rare that we agreed on anything. Nevertheless, because he was my father I respected him. Thankfully, before his death we came to terms with each other. We reached the point where we accepted one another as we were, and started down the road of actually enjoying each other's company. His death was definitely not a relief to me. He died a year after my mother's death under quite mysterious circumstances, and it was not from grieving for her. They had been divorced for about ten years when he died, and there had never been any indication from him that he missed her.

He was a methodical and the consummate planner. He did almost nothing spontaneously. After the divorce he married a woman with whom he had been in love during his early years of college, but back then when word got out that they wanted to get married his mother put an end to their aspirations.

When they did marry after the divorce from my mother, he was already a renal failure patient. Both his kidneys were doing nothing more than taking up space in his body, and so in order to remain alive he was dialyzed three times a week—his blood pumped out of his body, filtered and returned. The process took three to four hours each time. He told me more than once how much he hated the imposition and demands of his time for dialysis, but always ended with, "but you do what you have to do to stay alive."

Being a man of integrity, he made a point of ensuring his second wife knew of his condition so there would be no surprises. They got married fully anticipating that he would die long before her. When they had been married for no more than three or four years she quite unexpectedly discovered that she had a virulent cancer. In less than three months she was gone. Her death devastated my father. Despite his routine of going to work each day, he so withdrew from his previous social life that all his friends became concerned. He had trouble sleeping, and for years after her death he paced his apartment late at night talking out loud to her.

Then something happened. No one in our family ever figured it out, but suddenly he became interested in life again. I suspect that he either consciously or unconsciously knew his end was near, and perhaps that knowledge or intuition renewed a spark of life within him. At any rate, my older sister Nancy invited him to move to Brooklyn where he could live in the street-level apartment of her 7th Street brownstone near Park Slope. He seemed eager to recommence his life, and spoke of writing books and hob-knobbing with other writers in New York City. Because of his writing career he knew many of them and anticipated meeting and getting to know more.

Typically, he would plan out the entire operation in agonizing detail months in advance. He would go over his plans repeatedly until he was certain of every tiny step;

marketing and selling his apartment and possessions, ensuring his finances were in tip-top shape and determining what was the most financially wise way to make the changes he was planning for his life. However, in stark contrast to his normal behavior he quite suddenly sold his apartment, most of his possessions and summarily moved. Bang!

Before anyone knew what was going on, he moved to New York. Nancy said that when he arrived it was a joyous occasion. They were excited to see each other again and spent a day or two talking late into the night catching up. Then suddenly, almost literally overnight, his mind left him. He became someone my sister did not know. He screamed obscenities at her, accused her of all sorts of imagined offenses—that she was out to steal his things, that she was plotting and scheming against him, and so on—and he could not remember simple things like what had happened the day before. She quickly got him to a doctor. The hospital in Brooklyn admitted him, and he died there a few months later.

While he was under their care, the doctors vainly tried to determine what was wrong with him. Because he was a dialysis patient, the first thing they checked him for was AIDS. Negative. They ran test after test in fruitless attempts to determine the cause of his illness. They repeated the tests just to be sure of their results. Eventually, because they could not figure out what was happening to him, they simply started treating him for anything and everything. Nothing helped. When I went to see him in the hospital, he was naked and curled up in the fetal position without even a blanket or sheet over him. He was oblivious to his surroundings and unaware there were people nearby. As we left the hospital my parting comment to my brother in-law was, "He's never coming out of there alive." It was not a wish. It was a pronouncement. It was that obvious.

To this day, we still do not know why he died. He had been a heavy drinker most of his adult life, so we all imagined he likely had cirrhosis of the liver. The coroner quickly disproved that during the autopsy. My father had been on dialysis for over a decade. Perhaps it was just not doing the job of cleaning his blood of contaminants well enough anymore. After the autopsy, the medical examiner said my father could have lived at least another ten years based on the condition of his organs. His death certificate, however, stated that he died of "natural causes." They simply could not determine the true cause of his death.

To me, however, the oddest part about his death at the age of 65 was not the circumstances—although they were perplexing—but rather it was my response to his death. I grieved harder and longer over the loss of a man who had been so hard on me for so many years than I did when my mother died a year earlier. I knew my mother loved God and regularly attended church services, and while I could not equate any statement of hers to a salvation experience in her life, I knew she was a believer. I knew she was with Jesus. My father, on the other hand, was an avowed agnostic. More correctly, he was a die-hard humanist.

He believed we can pull ourselves out of all our problems by education and the strength of human will. Wars, poverty, hatred, and injustice—all the sins of the world man alone can solve. In his thinking, humanity is essentially good to the core. There is no "inherent sin," nobody is born flawed. At the very least, we are all—in his perspective—born no less than tabula rasa[7] (a clean slate) upon which society and environment write, thereby molding us into who we are as adults.

To our detriment, it is not popular in this post-modern society to speak of sin, much less to admit we are all born with a nature that rebels against God. This is what Christians refer to as our "sin nature." I firmly believe we are born sinners. In contrast, my father believed we are born good to the core.

In my father's eyes, Christian faith is for idiots, and anyone who believes in Jesus is not thinking clearly. To him, the church consists of liars, fools and charlatans with less than honorable intentions. He believed we could directly attribute all the nastiness of human history to religion of any kind and Christianity in particular. Granted, much evil has been done by humanity in the name of various religions, but the way I see it that only proves how deeply flawed and in need of saving we are and of how just and righteous is our God.

Like so many others, I struggled to understand why my father had died. It is, after all, only natural for us to try to wrap our mind around the death of someone we love. Beyond the obvious, we have an innate need to understand why those we love die. Whether we admit it or not, I believe that at some point we have to face the question "Isn't there more to life than this?" And it gnaws at us that one day we will die and will be the end of it all. (I do not believe that death is the end of life, but many people do.)

Sometimes those left behind turn their backs on God, mistakenly blaming him for their loved one's death. They become angry with God, wondering why he would allow that one to die. In a way, it is yet another of our attempts to be in control of something over which we have no control.

Sometimes God allows us to understand why a particular individual dies or why they died the way they did. At other times, in his infinite knowledge, he does not provide an explanation. More frequently, however, I think he brings us to the place where we are comforted by the Holy Spirit but without a full explanation. We do not like the not knowing, but the Comforter who comes makes it possible for us eventually to accept it.

As a Christian, I agonized over my father's death and questioned what became of the man who seemingly hated God and all I believed to be true. Was he in hell? Given his apparent life-long denial of God and anything associated with him, and especially his denial of Jesus Christ, I could not believe he could be in heaven. That being the case, I wondered about the seeming unfairness of it. If God loves us so much, why would he allow my father to go to hell? For that matter, why would he allow anyone to go to hell?

It has taken me years to come to the realization that if my father is in hell (and I am not yet convinced that he is) it is not God's doing. God does not send anyone to hell— each who goes there takes every step of the way his or herself. God is love and therefore does not force his will on us. He does not have to. He knows us better than we know ourselves. Because I am not my father, there is no way for me to really know if he ever did come to believe in the one true God or not, so I will not know of his state of being until I too have crossed from this life into the next. When he went to the grave, however, I am told he had a large picture of Jesus in his briefcase.

God was telling me something that was hard to accept: "It is not for you to yet know if your father is in heaven or in hell." In other words, he was saying to me that it is none of my business. Even though I did not like the answer, I now trust God enough to let it go at that.

I do have this much for which to be thankful; my father and I came to terms before his death. If he had died without our reconciling our differences, then I would be kicking myself for the rest of my life for having been so foolish. The short year or two that we had infrequent visits with each other were good years. I came to the point of accepting him as he was and of having a deeper respect and love for him. He came to the place of accepting me as an intelligent, maturing man.

On one occasion after my father's death, my older sister commented how she thought he had been unreasonably hard on me. To my surprise, rather than stirring up old bad feelings I came to his defense. I knew I had done many things late in my teens and in my early adult life that were foolish and had hurt him. Frankly, I still do foolish things. I knew that in his own way my father had tried to prevent me from making those mistakes because to one degree or another he had also made them. So, instead of bad mouthing him I defended him. What a change!

God had more to say to me about my father that I think applies equally to those who may have difficulty with one or both parents, a spouse, a sibling, a child, a boss, an employee, and so on. God said to me, "While you think about your father and your relationship with him over the course of your life, realize that you also have many problem areas, but I love and accept you anyway. You must therefore deal with others the same way I deal with you."

What God was saying to me—and I think also to all of us—is that we are neither to place conditions of acceptance on others, nor to try to justify our wrong responses. We are not, and cannot be responsible for what others think, say or do; but we certainly are responsible for our decisions, our words, our actions, our treatment and even our thoughts toward them. As the apostle Paul said in warning to the Roman Christians, it is only by the grace of God that any of us are saved. We therefore dare not have an exaggerated opinion of ourselves. Instead, we should think of others as more important, and soberly judge ourselves.[8] In other words, instead of thinking about the flaws, weaknesses or the failures of others we should think about how God loves us in spite of our own garbage.

In many ways I failed my father. I failed my mother too. I have failed my wife and my children. I have failed employers. I fail both God and myself daily. I regret my many failures, yet God accepts me just as I am and loves me anyway. Because of this, I have learned to accept myself. When I make a mistake, I admit it, and with his help get up and go on without feeling that the world is ending or that I am without any value. To the contrary, I now like me.

God wants us to love others the same way—just as they are. Do you long for freedom and peace from those who drive you up the wall, those who have hurt you, those who have broken your trust or your heart, or those who have let you down? Then stop trying to change them. Love them anyway. If God is not only willing to love them but desires to do so, then what right do we have not to love them as well?

That is not to say, however, that everything others do is okay. There are certainly times when we need to judge a person's behavior. The point I want to make here is that while we are to humbly love others and forgive them, there are behaviors with which we must deal. Emotional, mental, verbal or physical abuse is not okay. Lying and deceit are not acceptable either.

There are many things we do to each other that are not alright, many things we try to sweep under the rug until someone else does those very things to us. Then we want revenge, or "justice"—for God to intervene—meaning we want God to judge them instead of us getting our hands dirty. There certainly are times when we have to lay down the law to an abusive person. I am not one to say a wife or husband should tolerate an abusive spouse forever. That is the sort of foolishness that at best enables such a person to continue being abusive.

Their bad behaviors, however, do not justify our mistreatment of them. We do not have to bend over backwards to give them everything they want, but we do need to realize that we are not justified in God's eyes when we mistreat them. Justice and revenge are two very different things. We ought, instead, to pray for them, to look for ways to help them; and if all else fails, to release them to God.

The apostle Peter wrote to his fellow Christian Jews about all kinds of relationships. He warned them not to return evil for evil. When insulted we are not to reply in kind. Instead, we should be asking God's blessing for them, praying for their welfare, truly pitying and loving them. He tells us that this is what we are called to in order to inherit a blessing from God.[9] If you wonder what God's calling is for you, there is the answer: loving others and all the more so when they do you wrong.

While I cannot speak for others, I certainly want God's blessing and a heritage rather than judgment and condemnation. To get his blessing though, we have to bless others instead of cursing them. That does not mean one has to continue living with an abusive spouse, but neither does it grant us permission to be abusive in any manner in return.

The Death of Lucy

My sister, Lucy, lived a short and troubled life. The third of five children and slightly more than a year younger than I, she was born in 1953, and died at the age of 36. No one knows why or when her problems first began, but we all remember that she was quite troubled from an early age.

As a child she would frequently awaken in the middle of the night screaming like in a 50s horror movie. Today there is a term for it—night terrors—but back then we had no idea what was going on outside of the sudden hellish screams that erupted in the dead of night. People tell me that nightmares do not even come close to night terrors.[10] Thankfully, I do not have firsthand knowledge of that.

At any rate, our mother would rush to her and attempt to hold and comfort her. That only made things worse. It was many years later that we learned she had recurring nightmares about being trapped in a huge spider web, with a gigantic spider creeping toward her. Just as the spider was about to reach her she would wake up—at least we thought she had awakened—screaming, with our mother running in trying to pull her into her arms. In Lucy's mind, our mother's arms were the spider's legs.

As an adult, Lucy drifted in and out of alcoholism, in and out of drug abuse and in and out of almost every psychiatrist's office in town. They diagnosed her as manic-depressive and schizophrenic. This condition is known today as bipolar disorder.[11] One minute we could be laughing and joking with her, and the next minute she would shout obscenities and accuse us of all kinds of abusive behaviors. She could be on cloud nine one minute, and then in a heartbeat fall into a severe state of depression that might last for weeks. We never knew what to expect from her.

For many years after high school, Lucy remained living with our mother. I do not think she ever held a job. Every year or so, she would slit her wrists. After these suicidal episodes, she would spend a month or two in a state hospital. Inevitably, she would leave with more medications and feeling she had been heard.

After a few of these episodes and the subsequent medical attention, Lucy became adept at manipulating psychiatrists in order to obtain multiple prescriptions from them. She knew her pharmacology: exactly what to use, what not to use or mix with other medications and how to get them. Medicines had become her recreational escape. Drugs were not her only problem.

Her male friends were abusive. Most of them beat her. In the end, they all used her for their own gratification and then tossed her aside like so much garbage. Attitude and motivational speaker and author, Jeff Keller, says those with severe self-image problems seek out abusive people who reflect this poor self-image back onto them.[12] While I cannot address that with any level of expertise, it certainly appeared to be true of Lucy's attraction to abusive men. Whatever the cause, Lucy had more black eyes and bruises than anyone I have ever known. I never understood why she kept hooking up with such abysmal examples of manhood.

Then she met and married a man named Robert Smith. My immediate reaction to her engagement announcement was to joke with her that she could do better than going from Jones to Smith—and Bob Smith at that. Like Lucy, Robert was an alcoholic. Unfortunately, this is a common practice of alcoholics. High rates of alcoholic women marry alcoholic men. Sociologists call it assortative mating.[13] Together Lucy and Robert would climb on the wagon, and then fall off it. After a few years of frequent off and on drinking binges Robert came home one day, locked himself in their apartment, and proceeded to drink to the point that he died. As you can imagine, his death devastated Lucy.

Within a few weeks of Robert's death, she met a local evangelist pastor named Manny. After several conversations with Manny and his wife, Lucy decided that Jesus Christ is the real deal. She accepted that he died for her, that he arose from the dead, ascended to heaven and one day will return for her. Her life seemed to take a miraculous turn for the better. Full of anticipation and expectant joy, she was on the verge of moving to Oregon with Manny and his wife when her life came to a tragic end.

She spent her last weekend in Hawaii at the home of previous neighbors who appeared out of the woodwork three years earlier when my mother had died. They found her dead in one of their bedrooms, the result of a drug overdose. Police declared it a successful suicide, but I am not convinced that was the case. Peculiar circumstances surrounding her death suggested to both my older sister (an attorney) and me that Lucy's death was neither an accident nor a suicide.

She had received payment on her recently deceased Vietnam veteran husband's $100,000 life insurance policy and she still had almost all of it when she died. The couple with whom she was spending the weekend were penciled into her will the weekend that she died in their home. The wife had a serious and expensive medical complication. The prescription drugs that killed Lucy were provided to her by this same couple with whom she was staying and who had managed to get her to put them into her will that very weekend. I do not believe Lucy would ever have taken the combination of drugs that killed her. Drugs were not her way of getting attention; they were her recreation and her escape mechanism. The very day after her death, this couple began demanding to know when the will would be probated and when they would receive their share of Lucy's assets. In the end, they got away with a good amount of her money. Was it suicide? Not likely. Was it murder? I believe so.

This was a struggle for me for some time. I was quite understandably angry and bitter. I wanted them somehow to pay for my sister's death. Today, however, I no longer harbor bad feelings toward them. While what they did was criminal, I have no desire to be their judge. I think the hell they were going through with an unnamed and complicated illness and its attending medical bills likely placed a horrible strain on them. I pity them for such a struggle. That does not excuse what they did. I am not saying their actions were either justifiable or excusable. What I am saying is that I am not their judge. In the end they must answer to God. If they have confessed what they did and asked his forgiveness then I know he has forgiven them. If he will forgive them, then how can I not do so too? I ask for his blessings to be upon them.

Nancy, my oldest sister, asked me to write and deliver the eulogy for Lucy. I did so, and it was one of the most difficult things I have ever done. Despite my firm conviction that she was with Jesus, I could not hold back my tears through the service. I selected an instrumental song, "No Goodbyes,"[14] to play in her honor after the eulogy. For many months afterward, I could not listen to it without weeping in heaving sobs of anguish. So dramatic was the impact of her questionable death and my connection with the song played at her memorial service that to this day, nearly two decades later, I still "lose it" when I hear the tune.

What I learned through this trial was that even when we know someone we love also loves God, that does not mean we will not grieve the loss, nor should we pretend otherwise. At least we can hold to the promise that we will see them again one day. I know I will see Lucy again, and that combined with the comfort of a God who understands our sadness helped me to get through my grieving over Lucy's death.

By this point I was seeing a pattern and wondering why all this was happening to me, or more correctly to those whom I loved. Who would be next—my wife, my children, my brother or another sister? I have since lost both of my other two sisters: one to disease and the other to the results of years of alcoholism. I began to think that perhaps God was punishing me for the wicked things I had done. I was confused and filled with grief. One thing was certain: I had no real idea why these people I loved had died, and so I was beginning unconsciously to blame God.

It does not matter if a loved one's death comes suddenly or with lots of warning. When death comes, it is still a kick in the stomach. There are, however, those who have watched loved ones take years to die, and when death came, it was a relief. My point is that unless you have experienced it you cannot truly understand the feelings that come with death.

My favorite scripture for many years was "Jesus wept."[15] Perhaps you can see why. The story that leads up to that verse is about the death of Lazarus, Jesus' friend, and the brother of two women whom Jesus also loved. I believe he wept because he connected with the sorrow these sisters were experiencing over their brother's death. I do not think now, as I used to, that Jesus wept for Lazarus simply because he was his friend. I believe Jesus knew he was appointed to bring Lazarus back to life. I believe he wept because he felt and understood the pain he saw in Martha and Mary at their brother's death. In other words, he strongly connected with their grief. He fully empathized with them. He did not merely sympathize. He felt their grief. He felt their sorrow in their belief that Lazarus was gone forever.

The Death of Margaret

In the middle of writing this chapter, I had to deal with yet another precious loved one's death, that of my youngest sister, Margaret. She had medical problems for many years, and at some point in her early twenties doctors unfortunately misdiagnosed her with Lupus, a chronic autoimmune disease that can damage parts of the body such as skin, joints, and even internal organs.

Doctors are not gods, and even though they try very hard not to make mistakes, they are just as susceptible to making them as are the rest of us. I am sure they were doing their best for her, but unfortunately, they incorrectly diagnosed her condition. The subsequent off–and–on treatments so damaged her kidneys that she wound up like our father—on dialysis three times a week. For Maggie, this went on for close to twenty years.

Like my sister, Lucy, she never held a job for more than a week or two here and there. She spent much of her adult life as a ward of the state. Over the years Lucy and Margaret were so close and tight in relationship that they seemed to take turns being each other's shadow. I believe Lucy's death had a major impact on Margaret, one that she never got over.

Shortly after Lucy died, Maggie moved to Oregon, and for the next eighteen years, I had no idea of where she was other than somewhere in the northwest. I had no idea of how to reach her. I had no phone number, no address, nothing. Occasionally she would call Nancy, but from my vantage point, that was her only contact with the family.

Then one day I received an unexpected phone call from a number I did not recognize. Due to the nature of my work I was feeling somewhat stressed out, and did not answer the call. The caller left a message—one that came as a bit of a surprise—it was Maggie, and she left a phone number. She had called our brother and somehow heard a message I had left on his answering machine. My message contained my telephone number, which led her to call me. We had a wonderful conversation. Two weeks later, she was unconscious in a hospital due to infections resulting from pneumonia.

Nancy called late on a Monday night to tell me what was going on. By the following afternoon Maggie had died. At least she was not in any pain and did not hang in there for weeks or months. At the urging of the doctors, her caregiver and long time companion finally agreed to let them take her off life support systems. She went so quickly that they did not even have time to finish unplugging her before she was gone. Devastated by her death, her caregiver could not think straight, and so our oldest sister, Nancy, stepped in and managed the funeral arrangements and related business matters.

For me, Maggie's call a couple of weeks earlier was like a kiss on the cheek from God. It was as if he was saying, "I know she's about to die, so I'm going to get the two of you in contact again before then." That alone helped me to deal with her death. I am certain that my mother, and my sisters Lucy and Maggie, are all with our Lord today.

So there I was, again wondering why the people I so loved had died: first my mother from a protracted and painful cancer, a year later my father mysteriously of causes unknown, a year after that the murder of Lucy, and finally Margaret's death. I do not for even a moment believe God took them from me in order to teach me a lesson, but he did use their deaths to speak to and shape me in ways I would not have understood otherwise.

There is no way around it. When someone you love dies, it is extremely painful. It is devastating. Grief overwhelms you. This is natural and we ought to expect it. The good news is that if you will allow God to go through that painful place with you—as is his desire—you can go through grieving and come back to a life of purpose and fulfillment. Despite intense anguish over the loss of mother, father and sisters, I came through those experiences understanding better what others feel when someone they love dies.

This is not to say that God frivolously allows people to die just so we will understand how others feel. People die because we live in a fallen world, a world meant for God to control but in which we try to be in charge. We must come to where we can accept the tragedies in our lives, and go through the trials in ways that honor God and comfort those around us. The Bible tells us that he weeps with those who weep, and that he saves up every tear.[16] And so when a one of his children dies he grieves too.

Will I ever fully understand the timing and manner of their deaths? Probably not in this life, but today I am okay with that. I trust that God, who is even aware of the death of a sparrow, was there when each of these whom I love died. I trust that he loves them even more than I do—and certainly far more than a bird.

I realize there are some of you reading this who have experienced tragic deaths and simply cannot get over them. I will never even begin fully to understand the pain of you who have been forced to deal with gruesome or traumatic deaths. It is neither my intention to make light of them, nor in any way to demean their sorrow. Until we can release the death and every circumstance surrounding it to God, we cannot be at peace. Do we have the right to exact justice for wrongful deaths? Is it our place to determine the time, the place or even the way anyone dies? I think not. I believe God is the ultimate authority, the great judge, and one day the evil one will stand before him and answer for all these deaths. God will bring us vindication. When we try to do so, we are simply trying to usurp God's authority. He will not relinquish it to us. He is God and we are his creation.

Still, my heart called out to God the age-old question, "Why?" This time he spoke to me through scripture. The second king of Israel, David, wrote saying that God does not look upon the death of any of his loving ones as a light matter. We are precious in his sight.[17] Moses quoted the godly Job as having said, "... Naked (without possessions) came I [into this world] from my mother's womb, and naked (without possessions) shall I depart. The Lord gave and the Lord has taken away; blessed (praised and magnified in worship) be the name of the Lord! In all this Job sinned not nor charged God foolishly" (Job 1:21-22).

What was he really saying to me? God does not carelessly allow those who love him to die without purpose or at the wrong time. We may think otherwise, but our perceptions are not always right. Although we are often inconsistent or careless, God is not fickle in his dealings with us.

Today, as I sit here writing, it is Easter Sunday. As a Christian it is to me a day of tremendous significance. In fact it is the most important day of all. It is the day we celebrate the resurrection of Jesus Christ. Without the resurrection there is no point in Christian faith, there is no hope and there is no comfort in the death of anyone.

In the first century A.D., an extremely dysfunctional group of Christians in Corinth was teaching that there is no resurrection for any. Keep in mind that these people believed in Jesus; believed he was crucified, died, and came back to life three days later. The apostle Paul, correcting the false teachings, said in essence that if we only have hope in this life then we are the most miserable people on earth. We deserve to be pitied[17]. In other words, if Christ has not risen from the grave, then we have no hope of anything lasting. We are only wasting our time.

This is a very common and fatalistic view of life. For a time in the 90's an often-uttered mantra was, "Life sucks. Then you die." What a depressing outlook! If there was no resurrection, then those through the ages who loved Christ and have already died have perished—even in their Christian faith. Their faith was without value. It was empty. It had no meaning. If there is no resurrection then there is no point whatsoever in faith in Jesus Christ. Forget the struggle. Forget obedience to God. Forget God's love. Do whatever you please, because here and now is all you have. What a dismal outlook!

It is because of Christ's resurrection from the dead that I can look forward to seeing my mother, my sisters, and possibly my father again. It is the very reason I have the hope of life with the everlasting God. There is so much more to life than just the here and now. It is because of the resurrection that I can trust God's promises. Most importantly, it is because God, in Jesus Christ, has experienced the human and agonizing pain of death that I can be at peace about the deaths of those I love. He knows what it feels like. He knows firsthand the hurt, the suffering, the grief and the agony. That kind of God is a god whom I can trust and to whom I can relate. He knows my pain, my suffering, my grief. He has been there himself. He has personally experienced death in every way. He can empathize with me as can no other.

Our lives and our deaths are of utmost value to him. In the scripture quoted earlier about Job, all of his children had just died, all his wealth had just been stripped away and yet he did not foolishly blame God. He did not accuse God of killing his children or of destroying his wealth. He understood that God does not send death upon us or rob us. God does not put these painful trials on us, but he does allow and use them to make us people better suited to serve him. Satan is the one who comes to kill, steal and destroy.[18] Job instead accepted his horrendous losses as God's perfect will, putting into action his faith in God, trusting him to do what is right and best despite circumstances.

That is impossible for us unless we have a close relationship with God. That kind of trust does not come without having heard his voice in our darkest hours. It is in going through these crushing places that we learn to trust God. Listen for his living word—that which is his life giving voice—for it will bring comfort, encouragement, hope and a reason for living when you are in your deepest grief and despair.

As I have said already, the death of a loved one, or even dealing with our own impending deaths, is not easy. It is very difficult, agonizingly painful but not the end of everything of importance or value. It is death— nothing more, nothing less. Death is an eventuality for all of us. Scripture instructs us "… it is appointed for [all] men once to die, and after that the [certain] judgment" (Hebrews 9:27b). It is the first half of the two-part "certainties of life"—death and taxes. We do not have to like it. We do not have to long for it, but we really have no choice other than to endure it. If we are wise, we will trust God even in this place. As painful as the death of someone we love may be, it should remind us that there is still time for change. It should spark in us a need to examine the direction of our own lives.

At the time of editing this book, my oldest sister, Nancy, died at the age of 58. God carried me through her death as he has with that of every other one I have had to face, and he helped me to be a part of reconciling her children to her, sharing their grief with them. Even in death, we can experience victory. It is *not* the end.

SUBSTITUTE TEACHERS

You'll never know that Jesus is all you need
until Jesus is all you have.

Max Lucado

Feelings of inadequacy are something with which I have battled my whole life. While most of those feelings were, and are nothing more than our adversary falsely accusing me, some of them have been warranted. By far the biggest difficulty with which I had to deal in this chapter was publicly admitting to several of those mistakes, weaknesses and shortcomings that justifiably have caused me to feel like a failure. I confess them here because they came with lessons that may benefit you also.

This chapter is all about the things to which we turn instead of to God. I call them substitute teachers because when we should turn to God who best instructs us we instead turn to drugs, alcohol, food, sex, work, education, fitness, family, religion—anything but to God. These are substitutes for the real teacher—the Holy Spirit—and poor ones at that. If we will learn from our mistaken faith in these false hopes and false comforts, then God will use them to teach us rather than allowing them to remain the substitute gods we made of them.

When I was a teenager, I first turned to drugs. I was a child of the sixties, and peace, love and drugs were what it was all about. Well, at least it was for many. To a degree, I ran with that crowd. Some have tried to be funny by saying that if you can remember the sixties then you were not there. For a few that may be true, but it is not so for all. I was there, and I remember it. Pot was the drug of choice for most, and while I never became a chronic pothead, I did get high more than a few times. Hashish was another popular drug. The high from that was more intense and more costly.

Several of my friends were also "acid heads"—people who used LSD for its hallucinogenic effects. One of my best friends used to trip out in class. He would sit at his desk in our portable classroom, stare at the indoor-outdoor carpeting, and occasionally mumble, "Look at those patterns, man!" I swore never to use it. To me it just was not worth the risk. Thinking of the possibility of permanent brain damage scared me away.

And then one night, for reasons that still escape me, I caved in, dropped some acid and tripped out for the entire night. Most of that time was in my bed scared half to death. I felt the after effects for days. Years later I would still have little flashbacks from it, but fortunately nothing that lasted more than a few seconds. Even in my late fifties, I have phosphene[1] episodes now and then. I thank God that lifestyle is far behind me now. I never realized my biggest fear of deformed children. I have two sons and two daughters, now all adults, who were born perfectly normal and grew up, as Garrison Keillor said about Lake

Wobegon, "where all the women are strong, all the men are good-looking, and all the children are above average."[2] Sometimes, however, when I cannot remember something, or have a little difficulty grasping an idea, I still wonder if it is the result of the drugs. My wife says I'm just old, but I'm not giving in. That's my story, and I'm sticking to it.

While still in high school, and continuing for a couple of years later, I became involved in the occult in both thought and practice. It all started out innocently enough, but against my will it did not take long before it drew me in completely. While there are some hocus-pocus kinds of people who pretend and use contrived abilities to take advantage of the ignorant, or merely to entertain, it is not all make believe.

Based on personal experience I say there is real power there. Do not think for a moment that it is all silliness or just people whose heads are not on straight. Fakirs in India do walk on water. Even the Bible records how Pharaoh's magicians up to a point mimicked the miracles God performed through Moses and Aaron. There most assuredly are dark powers at work in this world, and none of them are here for yours or anyone else's betterment. Do not be fooled.

In my ignorance, I thought there was such a thing as white magic in contrast to black magic (or good and evil magic) and in the right use of such power versus the wrong use. I could not have been more wrong. It is all black. It all comes from Satan. I have experienced firsthand how a seemingly innocent séance or playing with a Ouija board can quickly pull a person into the occult.

In my case, it started with only a minor interest in a book on magic that I came across in my high school library. It was nothing more than dabbling, but before I knew it, I was using tarot cards and accurately telling people things about themselves that no one else could possibly have known. I studied incantations and later lived in the same house with a practicing warlock who held coven meetings in his locked room. I foolishly aspired to be in the same place as he—only I thought I was going to be practicing white magic instead. Yeah, right.

It should come as no surprise that, bound up with these occult dealings, is drug use. The two go together. In fact, the source word for what we now call witchcraft is the same root word for pharmacology—the mixing of drugs.

It was not long before I began to see the ugly side of the occult, but by then I was powerless to extricate myself from its deadly grip. This may sound crazy to those who have never been there, but in late 1970 I was twice chased by a demon. They were the most frightening experiences of my life. The first time it happened while I was on my way home from work.

Suddenly I felt an evil presence. The best that I can describe the sensation is that it was a sense of imminent and deep foreboding that I could not deny. I knew immediately what it was. Do not ask how. There is no logical explanation. I just knew. I drove my motorcycle at full speed all the way home, down the steep driveway and rushed into the house to seek help from my "friend" the warlock. Whatever it was that was chasing me did not come into the house. It shook me to the core. Literally quaking and lamely inhaling cigarette after cigarette in a vain attempt to calm myself, I explained to the warlock what had transpired. He immediately called his fellow witches and warlocks to a coven meeting. There was some talk of inducting me as a witch that night, but thankfully it did not happen.

I expect some will think it was all just my imagination, or the effect of too many experiments with drugs, but I know it was real. I was not looking forward to the experience, and am sure it was not something I just cooked up in my head. I did not wake up that morning saying, "You know, Gardiner, I just have this premonition that a demon is going to come after you today." I certainly was not wishing for it either. I had not used any drugs—not even aspirin—for quite a while before the episode.

The second encounter happened a few days later while I was on my way to work. This time, however, I blacked out. That is the only way I know to describe it. To this day, there is a gap in my memory. I do not know what happened other than I felt that same evil presence rushing up on me, and I took off as fast as I could go. I still do not know what happened next, but I found myself many miles away, in the opposite direction from which I had been headed and without an inkling of how or why I got there. Sitting here now it all sounds so insane, but I assure you at the time it was quite real to me. I have no doubt that there are evil spiritual forces at work in this world today. They have been here for a very long time.

In his famous passage of instruction on putting on all of the spiritual armor that God provides us, the apostle Paul first tells us why we need to put it on. He gave us the reason to heed him and then the instructions to follow. He said we are not struggling with physical opponents. Our fight is with powers, spirits, rulers of darkness and wickedness in the supernatural sphere.[3] Oh yes, they are out there, and if you give them so much as a toe hold they will latch on to you and drag you down.

Into this foolish combination of drugs and the occult I added another substitute teacher: image. I wanted to be bad. Well not really bad, but I did want people to look at me and think, "Whoa. That's one bad dude." I idolized bikers, and I do not mean the kind with pedals and baskets. Peter Fonda and Dennis Hopper epitomized my heroes of the time in their 1969 film, "Easy Rider."[4] For me, anyone on a chopper (a motorcycle, most commonly a Harley Davidson, stripped of anything unnecessary) was too cool for words. My ambition then was to ride a chopper and to become a Harley Davidson mechanic. I achieved both goals but at quite a cost.

When I finished high school, instead of going to college I ran off to Los Angeles on a wild goose chase and had to return home a month later with my tail between my legs. A high school buddy of mine talked me into going with him to promote a rock and roll band, and we wound up staying in a motel in Watts a mere two years after the infamous riots. I carried a large knife in my boot because it was not a safe place for a white boy like me. The friend I went there with was arrested on Hollywood Boulevard when he tried to sell some mescaline to a narcotics officer, and I wound up on the streets with no money, no job, no shelter, no food and nowhere to go.

God must have been looking out for me because while my friend was being arrested I was at a "Jesus Freak" church service. I will not lie and say I was there because I wanted to be in church. I was there because they promised me a warm meal after the service. I did not stick around for the meal. Their behavior so freaked me out that I did not want to stay. I thought they were crazy. They were raising their hands in the air, weeping, jumping up and down, dancing; and worst of all, babbling. Today I raise my hands in praise, tears will roll down my face, and sometimes I even jump up and down. Back then, that was all too strange for a young man accustomed to liturgical church services.

So there I was, alone in a huge city. I did not know where to go or what to do. I can still recall the day there when, after wandering the streets alone for two days, I ate two very green grapefruit off a tree in someone's yard. I was so hungry that they actually tasted good.

I finally realized I needed help from someone, and the only place I could think of to get help—as much as I did not want to—was from my parents. Faced with the harsh realities of life I came to my senses and made a collect call home. My parents were gracious enough to pay for a one-way ticket from San Francisco back to Honolulu. I hitchhiked from Los Angeles up to San Rafael north of San Francisco to my aunt and uncle's home where I stayed a few days before flying back home to Hawaii.

I felt crushed. After six blissful months of living on my own (I had moved out the day after I graduated from high school), I was forced to move back into my parents' house. I entered a community college but not for getting a real education. I simply wanted to get some auto mechanics courses under my belt so that the local Harley Davidson dealership would consider me for an entry-level job as a mechanic. It worked. The summer following my fiasco in Los Angeles, I became a Harley mechanic. It was a dream come true, but it also came with a healthy reality check. Other than being allowed to actually work on Harley Davidson motorcycles it was simply hard work, and the money was only a hair above minimum wage—hardly enough to support myself on much less to get married and start a family.

A short time later, the motorcycle of my dreams came into my life. A sailor from Pearl Harbor sold a 1952 "Panhead" chopper to the shop for $300. He probably had to ship out that very day because it was certainly worth more than that. I had seen this bike a year before and had wanted it from the day I saw it. With upswept megaphone exhaust pipes, a tall sissy bar, a 21-inch front wheel raked and extended and a "peanut" gas tank painted up with a rebel flag. It said "bad" all over. It was sort of a Southern version of the chopper, Captain America, which Peter Fonda rode in "Easy Rider." The difference, however, was that it was not as clean as Captain America. Fonda's bike was all polish, chrome and shine. This one was what bikers refer to as a rat bike—one that is not clean and likely has lots of spray paint on it. In short, it was the opposite of a show bike. It looked like it had been ridden hard a lot. To make it even cooler it had a foot clutch and hand shift—both on the left side of the bike—known as a suicide or Pasadena clutch. At one time, it had been a police motorcycle with a sidecar, which is why it had a stick shift with three gears forward and one for reverse. I loved it.

After my boss had me strip the paint off it, I could not take it anymore. I asked the shop owner if I could buy it, and he agreed to sell it to me for $600—a fortune to a 19 year old on minimum wage in 1971. I needed a promissory note in order to finance it. My dad refused to co-sign, so I went behind his back and managed to talk a police officer friend into co-signing. I got my bike. My dad was furious with me, but I did not care. "Big Bertha" was mine.

Next came joining the motorcycle club called the Sons of Hawaii. Hardly anyone outside of Hawaii knows of them, but at the time they had quite a reputation. When the Hell's Angels tried to start a chapter in Honolulu in the late sixties, the Sons of Hawaii beat them badly enough that they left and never returned. I thought I was in heaven. I was working as a Harley Davidson mechanic, I rode a chopper, and I was in a club. I was literally in Hog heaven! But, I had alienated my father further and had wasted two years of my life chasing the wrong dream. I am not saying that motorcycles or those who ride them are going down the wrong road, but I had completely bought the lie about being a bad boy biker. It was an attempt to be my own god, and I foolishly thought I was being cool when what I was actually being was foolish. I could have been halfway through college when my world turned upside down.

In January of 1972, my lottery number for the military draft came up 17. Either I was going to enlist or the Army would take me and send me to Vietnam. There was not any way I was going to enlist in the Army or the Marine Corps, so that left the Navy and the Air Force. Rather than speaking just to recruiters, I went and spoke directly with the sailors and airmen at Pearl Harbor and Hickam Air Force Base. I took the battery of aptitude tests and recruiters told that because of my scores they could guarantee just about any job I wanted. Both the Navy and the Air Force had excellent technical training—skills for jobs that could be used after a hitch in the military—but the airmen I spoke with sounded as if they were treated a little better so I signed up with the Air Force to become an "Avionic Inertial and Radar Navigation Systems Repairman." I had no idea what that meant, but it sounded the very impressive and that was all I needed to make my choice.

The Air Force did a good job of straightening out my desire to have a bad image. The shock of that first morning wake-up in boot camp is something I will never forget. I vividly recall the banging of metal trashcan lids at "O'-Dark-Thirty" and the sound of the drill sergeant's shout, "Get up! Get out of bed! Fall OUT!" My first semi-conscious thought was "What have I gotten myself into?" which was quickly followed by a mournful, "Oh ... my ... God!"

During basic training, the Air Force allowed us each a pass to go into San Antonio for one day. We poured onto the busses with visions of beer and girls. I somehow wound up at the Christian Servicemen's Center. Coincidence? I think it was God. As I expected, a man came up to me and asked if he could talk with me. I knew he was going to flap his gums at me about Jesus. I thought, "Well, if he wants to waste his breath then that's his problem. I'll just smile and nod my head, and then leave."

Oddly enough, the more he talked the more I felt compelled to listen. Something inside of me wanted to hear more even though my head was screaming, "Get out!" Before I left, I had accepted Jesus. That means I admitted I am a sinner and in need of a Savior. I attested that Jesus Christ is the Son of God, born of a virgin, suffered and died; was buried, resurrected, and ascended into heaven. I confessed these things and asked him to forgive me for my sin and to become my master, my Lord.

Now, I do not mean to crush some Christian teachers' ideas about salvation, but my chasing after false gods and substitute teachers did not end in 1972. The changes he brings will take all of my lifetime here. What did immediately end, however, was the stronghold that the occult had on me. It was forever broken. I learned my first lesson from God: he is bigger than everyone and everything, and I will never be able completely to comprehend him. God is so hugely mysterious that I will never be able to put him into a box.

Years later, thinking that I was a solidly grounded Christian husband and father, I discovered once again what an idiot I could be. I was still thinking that I could do it all. In church circles we call that a works-mentality. It essentially believes that we can become deserving of God's blessings by what we do, and that we can keep ourselves clean in God's eyes by our own efforts. Jesus condemned the same thinking in the Pharisees.

Only God's mercy and grace enable us to receive anything from him. When we have faith good works ought to follow us, but it is not our works that save us. My mindset of being able to be completely in control of myself found not just a toehold but a stronghold in me. That is all it usually takes: just a tiny bit of ground relinquished to the enemy. We must decide to change, but it is God who brings about change in us once we submit to his will, his hammer and his chisel.

I returned to smoking cigarettes. That is not necessarily an evil thing, but it is certainly something that was harmful to me and offensive to others. I also started drinking a lot of scotch whiskey, and eventually ran off for a woman, leaving my wife and two sons behind. Some Christian! Some would say because of that, I was never really "saved." That is not true. Any of us are just as susceptible to falling as hard as did I. That is why the Bible exhorts us to guard our hearts.[5]

As horrible as that sounds—and it was indeed a wicked and horrible thing for me to do—it turned into one of the best lessons of my life. I learned how weak I am. I learned how gracious and forgiving our God is. I learned what a fool I had been to think I would never do anything like that, and I learned so much more than I can ever fully describe about the value of my wife. The week that I left, her father told her, "He's never coming back." That was not exactly helpful to her. Jesus became her husband for nearly two years while I was in Massachusetts and she and our sons were in Hawaii.

During those two years, I tried with all my power to turn my back completely on God and my family. Thankfully, he never let go of me. He let the rope play out so that I would learn the hard way. By my behavior, I figuratively ran to the end of the rope, only to choke when it yanked me back. This choking usually came as the nagging thought about my responsibility to my sons. More scotch and more irresponsible behavior usually followed. I still was not learning.

Then one night I awoke with a start. In an instant I was sitting, bolt upright in bed, screaming at the top of my lungs, "NOoooooo!" I had just experienced the most vivid nightmare of my life. In this dream, my seven-year old son died in my arms. The hammer and chisel hit harder. This was the beginning of my wake-up call from God. Over a period of a few months I came to my senses, realized how precious my sons were and how important it was for me to be there, day-in and day-out. Coupled with this growing sense of undeniable responsibility was the realization that I wanted my family after all, and that not only was my wife vital to our family's success she really was the one woman I loved. It was dawning on me in that "oh my God, I wish I could undo this terrible mess" sort of way that she was far more valuable to me than anyone or anything.

Would she take me back? Was there even a chance she would ever allow me back in her life after what I had done? I hoped, but I did not pray. Then I made the call. At that point, reconciliation was not something she desired. Yet while I had been shoving my thumbs into my ears trying to keep from hearing God, she had been listening to his voice. She conceded, and I moved her and our sons to New England. The path before us was going to be long and difficult, but I believed both that we could make it and that it was worth the effort. Do you see what I was doing? I was still thinking that I could do this, that I had the power to fix things. God was not even on my radarscope.

Every Sunday morning my wife took our sons to church. I did not complain about it, but I did not go with them either. I told her that was okay with me, but I also told her I would tell them that I believed there is no God, and they could decide for themselves. Every now and then, I would attend a "non-church" event like a summer ice-cream social at the pastor's home, but I never went to a worship service. I had no desire to take part in something in which I did not believe. I could not commit to something I did not believe. It had to be a case of all of me or none of me.

On more than one occasion a couple of men from the church ganged up on me in the kitchen and literally poked their fingers into my chest, reminding me of my responsibility to be a godly father to my children. Each time after they had made their best arguments, they would conclude with, "So, will we be seeing you in church this Sunday?" They always received the same reply, "Maybe," and nothing more. I am sure it frustrated them, but in hindsight, I am thankful they did not give up. Their persistence and God's patience paid off.

A couple of years later I began going to church services again, but by then it was because I wanted to be there. God had slowly and lovingly brought me back around to where I believed again and wanted to get close to him once more. The change was not the result of going to church services, reading the Bible or anything related. People were praying. And, ladies, I think a big part of my coming back to God was due to my wife not beating me over the head about how I needed to be with her in church. I knew that it hurt her that I was not interested in God, and I am sure she wanted to scold me about my lifestyle. Instead, she let the Holy Spirit work on me. She let her godly behavior speak to me louder than any words she could have uttered. She will also be the first to tell you, "It was a tough time."

In the most loving way I can imagine, God allowed me to make a total mess of my life, and then he let me walk around like a blind man in the dark. Ever so slowly—because he knew that was what it would take with me—he brought more and more of his truth back into my life until I clearly saw the certainty of his existence and of my undeniable need of him.

I have gone to these extremes of storytelling in order to bring it around to this: nothing you can do will make God let go of you. There is nothing too terrible, horrible, wretched or sinful you can do that will prevent him from taking you back. It is because of the wicked things I did that I have a heightened awareness of my own potential for evil and of God's transcendent mercy, grace and love.

When I come into his holy presence, I cannot help feeling tarnished by my sin. For a long time I had difficulty dealing with the tears that would stream down my face when I felt again the horribleness of my own sin and the tremendous love of God for me. They no longer embarrass me. To me they are a gift from heaven. I take great joy in the Holy Spirit's reminders of his love and mercy. It keeps me humble and in awe of him.

We are all so easily and stealthily drawn to these substitute teachers. If not for hearing God's whisperings of love, if not for his all-knowing use of hammer and chisel, we would each continue down these paths of our own choosing to our destruction. Today, at a moderately advance age, much of my own wicked past and the allure of so many substitute teachers are far behind me. However, I also know how easily I can still be enticed down the wrong path. Therefore I am aware of how much I must daily depend upon God to keep me on the right course.

So exactly what has God been saying to me all these years through my times of wandering off course? He has thankfully been gracious enough often to remind me of how fragile my hold is on this thing we call holiness. I know, and am frequently reminded, that it is neither by my own strength nor any authority anyone else grants to me that I can spend even one minute—never mind one hour—in right standing with God. It is only because of Jesus' completed work on the cross that I am ever able to do so.

In chapter 3 of the book of Zechariah in the Old Testament, there is an out of the ordinary verse in the middle of his prophecy about Jerusalem and the rebuilding of the temple after the Israel's captivity in Babylon. There is a major lesson in that whole story about the captivity in

Babylon that I will not go into here, but I do encourage you to study it on your own. Seemingly out of nowhere, Zechariah refers to the high priest, Joshua. Remember him? He picked up where Moses left off and entered into the Promised Land. Speaking of this holy man, this high priest, Zechariah says in verses three and four:

"Now Joshua was clothed with filthy garments and was standing before the Angel [of the Lord]. And He spoke to those who stood before Him, saying, Take away the filthy garments from him. And He said to [Joshua], Behold, I have caused your iniquity to pass from you, and I will clothe you with rich apparel" (Zechariah 3:3-4 AMP).

Do you hear what God is saying? It is both a judgment and a whisper of love. He says, "I see your dirty clothes"— our wrong lifestyles with these substitute teachers. He does not candy-coat the truth of our sin. He does not excuse it, or as we do try to explain it away. He would not be just if he did. He also does not leave us condemned by our own sin. In the same breath he said, "… but look at the clean ones I have put you into." Instead of our own filthiness, our impotent attempts to be holy and even our outright sin, he has clothed us with the very righteousness of Jesus, the only one on earth who ever lived a sinless life.

In the next chapter of Zechariah, Zerubbabel—a man in a very tight spot and seriously in need of encouragement— receives a word from the Lord. The King James Version of the Bible puts it, "… Not by might, nor by power, but by My spirit … says the Lord of hosts" (Zechariah 4:6 KJV). The great apostle Paul said as both an explanation and a warning, "[Not in your own strength] for it is God Who is all the while effectually at work in you [energizing and creating in you the power and desire], both to will and to work for his good pleasure and satisfaction and delight" (Philippians 2:13 AMP).

None of the things we turn to will get us there. None of our own efforts will lead us into holiness, but if we will heed the leading of the Holy Spirit then he will clothe us with his righteousness. Forget the substitute teachers. I want the president of the college. Give me the Holy Spirit as my teacher!

SUFFERING INJUSTICE

"Be true to your heart."
Now that will really *get you into trouble!*

Suffering injustice is something with which I believe everyone can identify. It is also one of the few things that can be biblically justifiable cause for anger. It is the one thing about which we most often complain, and yet of which Christ told us not to complain. That is a tall order in a world filled with injustice, especially when so often the cry of our heart is "Why?"

"That's not fair." We have all said it, and if we have not said it then we have at least thought it. Even children learn early on to decry their perceived injustices. When one sibling gets to go somewhere and the other must stay home the cry is raised, "But, mom! That's not fair!" If one child gets to stay up later at night, then brother or sister will cry, "That's not fair!" Adults do the same thing. "Why didn't the cop pull that other guy over too?" "How come he got a pay raise and I didn't?" Often the complaint is accurate, because the hard truth is that life is not fair.

Not too surprisingly, injustice is also one of the reasons some give for not believing in God. They question how a

God who is supposed to be loving and good could allow evil and injustice to exist. The thinking is because evil and injustice do exist there cannot be a God. I have asked it, and I am willing to bet you have too. When your best friend, who could never hurt a soul, calls to tell you the doctors have told her she has cancer you will ask why God allows it. When a gentle and God-loving person dies in a fatal accident but the drug dealer or the murderer continues to live a pleasant life, you will ask why God allows such things to continue. We question God because these things are unjust, and God is supposed to be the epitome of justice.

While some may use that as an excuse for not believing in God, there are those who honestly struggle with the question. Even those strong in faith sometimes wonder about this while in the thick of life's trials. If you are honestly looking for an answer, I recommend Ravi Zacharias's book, "Cries of the Heart: Bringing God Near When He Feels So Far." Ravi does an excellent job of tackling the issue. One of his comments struck home with me. He said, "When you are looking for wisdom, always look for one who has suffered much but whose faith has remained unshaken." While we may question God for allowing injustice to continue, there are reasons he allows it that we can sometimes understand. Even in our worst nightmares, he has the ability to bring good things to us.

Accepting that God allows injustice was one of my hardest lessons. Like you, I do not like unjust suffering. It also makes me angry. Many of us have to learn the hard way that suffering injustice is one of God's biggest chisels. I am not saying that he desires for us to suffer and hurt. He does not. His desire for us is always for our best. However, he does use our suffering to sculpt us. It is through our limited understanding of the character of God and in learning to trust in him—instead of in ourselves, others or our circumstances—that he carries us through times of suffering injustice, helping us to yield ourselves more to his hammer and chisel. In return, we reap wisdom and stronger faith.

Injustice is everywhere, and the cry of those suffering is usually for vindication. We naturally want whatever injustice we are going through to end, and we want the person we think is the cause of it to receive just recompense. In other words, we want them to pay. Many have reason to long for help and relief from injustice. Nearly every one reading this is in the middle of suffering some sort of injustice, has had to bear it in the past, or at least knows someone whose heart cries out because of it.

I too have had to endure some painful injustices, but I have learned through enduring them something that does not come without trial. When faced with a situation we cannot resolve ourselves, we can take the low road and seek escape, retribution or vengeance, or we can take the high road—allowing God to chisel us—and trust his faithfulness.

About 30 years after the crucifixion of Jesus, the apostle Paul wrote a letter to the Christians living in Philippi where he had some years earlier established the first church in Europe. He wrote to them from a very unhappy place—a Roman prison. Paul had faced the kinds of injustice that many of us would do everything in our power to avoid. While he had lived in great wealth at one time, he had also lived in abject poverty; been unjustly accused, beaten and stoned so horribly that his assailants left him for dead. He had been both shipwrecked and imprisoned more than once,[1] and yet Paul wrote this letter to the Philippians while he was filled with joy! How could that be? Paul had learned the difference between happiness and joy. How many of us could express joy in the middle of our worst nightmares of injustice?

We naturally want to be happy, and we will go to extremes in our elusive search for it. In the United States of America, our Declaration of Independence even states that we have a God-given right to pursue happiness. We will spend countless hours and large sums of money trying to find it. We will seek it in new experiences, in collecting material goods, in a variety of relationships, and so on.

In the midst of our search we fail to consider what happens when our house of cards comes crashing down: when all our shiny toys have rusted, when those we love die, when our wealth evaporates, when our health tanks out, when we lose our jobs, when we have reached the end of the line, when life falls apart around us. When these things happen, we more often than not fall into despair. I do not think it is coincidental that so many people suffer from clinical depression and require medication to maintain some sort of emotional equilibrium. For example, 10 years ago the National Health Institute of Mental Health reported that more than 19 million Americans suffer from clinical depression every year.[2]

The reason we so often hurt is that the circumstances of our lives are not bringing us the happiness for which we long. I understand this feeling of hopelessness. I have been there and will be again. I have lost loved ones to disease and murder. I have lost my job multiple times. I have had to deal with serious health complications for children with no way in sight to pay for treatment or medications. I have nearly lost my wife more than once. I have been arrested and in jail. And if all of that is not enough, I have been shot at as well. If you are in this place of feeling helpless and hopeless, my heart goes out to you. Know that there is hope.

Joy, on the other hand, is a quiet and confident assurance of God's love for us, which we base on his faithfulness to work everything out in our lives for the best. Joy does not depend on circumstances. We may be hurting yet still have joy. It has been my experience that God is there with us through all our trials, and that in the end there will be his just vindication. This cannot be head knowledge alone. Coming to understand this truth requires walking through the fires of injustice. That, I believe, is what moves the knowing from our heads to our hearts. Someone said that happiness depends on happenings, but joy depends on Christ. I like that way of putting it, and I will add that joy is more than an emotion. It is a quality that is grounded in—and even comes from—God himself. It should characterize the life of Christians.

It is only natural for us to want our lives to be smooth, unruffled, without problems or disturbances. When it is not, we complain to anyone who will listen—to others, to

God and more often to both. Sadly, some Christians tell people that when they come to know Jesus all their problems end. That could not be further from the truth, and those who have promoted this belief have done far more harm than good. Even Jesus told us that we would have problems.[3]

The reason is that when you become a Christian you are no longer part of this world. You belong to God, and that puts you at enmity with the world. And yet, many of us still believe that if we just try hard enough we can find happiness on our own. We buy into the lie that if we work hard enough and become "successful" (whatever that really means); or if we care about others enough, if we pray enough, if we are good enough, if we just dig in and ride it out then we can find happiness. That may work for you, but it will do so only for a short while. It does not last because it depends on circumstances rather than on trusting God in all things.

Never have I met a person who had it all together, who walked a perfect, tranquil, flawless life. While I have met some very strong people—both Christians and non-Christians, some of whom looked like they really had their act together—even they had their problems. Where most of us err is in expecting God immediately to make everything better for us whenever something goes wrong, to immediately correct any perceived injustice the moment we complain to him about it. When he does not fix things the way we think he ought to, or in the timeframe we expect, then in our hearts we pout and say, "That's not fair," or we go out in the yard, scream, and shake our fists at him as I once did.

You will not hear me foolishly suggest that God is the author of the bad things in our lives. Many of our problems are of our own making, but certainly not always. Sometimes others do things to us. At other times, life just falls in around us. Accidents happen—that is why we call them accidents. People die in fatal car wrecks every day, and it is often because of something someone else did behind the wheel. God does not cause those accidents.

We cannot justifiably relegate all of our sufferings to the will of God, the will of man, or even to our own foolishness. Life is full of rough edges. It is dangerous and even exciting because of its harshness. Sometimes we deserve what happens to us, and other times we do not. That is simply life, and there is no getting around it.

We can also easily confuse suffering injustice as punishment from God. Many think either consciously or unconsciously that when things go wrong it is God punishing them. While that may be true on occasion, it happens a lot less frequently than many think. God loves to forgive and restore. All suffering is not God's punishment. That is a lie from the pit of hell. Just one simple example is enough to show that teaching is wrong. Do any of us seriously believe that God came up with the idea of crack babies so he could punish the parents?

When God does punish it is always just and perfect, and while it may not fit well with our ideals, that does not make his punishments unjust. Perhaps where we disagree with him we need to get our vision more in line with his. For example, our fathers disciplined us, and I am sure none of us liked that, but it was for our good. The same is true with God, only he does not unjustly punish us as some fathers or mothers may, and his correction is always for our certain good.[4]

We sometimes confuse our suffering as punishment when it is not. Religion—man's attempts to be righteous yet failing miserably to meet God's standards—plays a big part in that sort of incorrect thinking. More often, what we see as punishment is just our accuser, Satan, masquerading as both judge and jury in our lives.

What can be so difficult for us to accept is that God allows bad things to happen to us because he loves us. That can be a bitter pill to swallow, so let me try to explain what I mean. Scripture tells us in Romans 8:28 (AMP), "We are assured and know that [God being a partner in their labor] all things work together and are [fitting into a plan] for good to and for those who love God and are called according to [His] design and purpose." Let's break that down and examine it a bit more closely.

The phrase "we are assured" should be a source of consolation for us. It reminds us that all things are under the direction of an infinitely wise God, one who has appointed everything. Chaos does not rule our lives if we love God.

"All things" is, by definition, all-inclusive. It means not just the good in life, but our trials as well. The hard places we go through may be many and long lasting, but they are one of the means he uses for our benefit.

"Work together and are for good," means that in combination they contribute to our good. Each piece, each trial works in concert with everything else in our lives for our betterment. They help us to stop looking at the world as our source of goodness or happiness. They teach us the truth about our frail condition in this world. They lead us to look to God for support. They produce a subdued spirit, a humble temper; a patient, tender and kind disposition.[5]

God will use our problems to teach us, to mold us, to break us but he never puts them on us. As R. T. Kendall, pastor of Westminster Chapel in London for 25 years said, "Only a fool would claim to know the full answer to the question, 'Why does God allow evil and suffering to continue when he has the power to stop it?' But there is a partial answer: he does so in order that we may believe. There would be no need for faith if we knew the answer concerning the origin of evil and the reason for suffering. I only know that it is what makes faith possible."[6]

Well, I will say it again: life is not fair. We may as well get used to it. The bottom line is that God can and does use everything in our lives, including the bad, to bring about his perfect purposes for us.

Things are never seemingly perfect for very long. What I have discovered as a Christian is that when everything is going smoothly I need to be actively on guard. It usually means something in my life is not right. It tells me that in some area I have given the enemy a foothold.

The Holy Spirit brought this home to me one day while driving to work. As is often my habit, I was taking the time to cry out to God. I was feeling upset that day about some things that were going wrong in my life, and so I was being less than spiritually minded. Translation: I was complaining to God about my problems, and telling him I thought he was not being fair by allowing them to continue. I was sulking before the throne of God. I was frustrated and whining to him about bills and car problems. Finally, I received an unexpected response. He said, "That's right. I'm not fair, and you should be glad that I'm not."

What I wanted to hear was, "Oh my poor son, you have suffered so much. Let me take care of all these problems for you right now." That was not what he had to say. For me it was a revelation. What any of us deserve is hell and damnation, and yet what we receive is grace and mercy from the hand of a just, a righteous and a loving God.

Was he literally saying that he is not fair in his dealings with us? Of course not. He was telling me that I was not seeing things correctly; my perception was off, my focus was wrong. I was once again caught up with my own ideas and perceptions, still clinging to my own mindset.

There is much truth in the popular line, "What goes around comes around." Even the Bible tells us that we sow what we reap.[7] While I will not offer excuses for my wrong behavior; and while I am a man who loves God and who feels a deep and intimate connection with him, I am also a human being who still has to cope with my natural tendency when left to myself to do the wrong thing instead of what is right. Like everyone else, I make mistakes. Sometimes those mistakes are intentional. More often, they are accidental. Honestly, I trip up every day. We all do.

When I fall, I confess my failure to God, and I get back up to go on. You can too. King Solomon said a righteous man may fall often, but he keeps getting back up.[8] I find it comforting to know we can get back up when we fall, don't you? Even the pillar of the early Church, the apostle Paul, said that when he intended to do good things he failed to do them, yet when he vowed not to do what was wrong he went ahead and did it anyway.[9] Man, I can identify with that!

Another good example is King David. The Bible refers to him as "a man after God's own heart,"[10] and yet he failed miserably more than just once. This godly man committed adultery with Bathsheba, had her husband killed and then tried to cover it all up. Knowing that, would you call him a man after God's own heart?

David was supposed to have this wonderful relationship with God, so it makes me wonder what the phrase "a man after his own heart" means. I do not think it means that David was a pristine mirror of God's heart. I believe it means God understood David's heart, that he knew David wanted God's will to rule his life. He knew David would do what he asked of him. David might fail like the rest of us, but he would come around again.

In our eyes, it is easy to focus on how he so miserably failed God's trust, but despite David's failures God forgave and restored their relationship. He did have to admit his wrongful behavior (his sin), turn from it, and seek God's forgiveness. Even then, he still reaped the consequences of his actions. David knew he had grossly sinned. He was also keenly aware that the ugliest part of his offense was that he had violated God's law.

Bringing it home, the message here is that God will forgive and restore even someone we may not want living next door to us. This adulterer, murderer, deceiver went on to become one of the direct human ancestors of Jesus. His sin did not hold him back because his heart was quick to confess and to seek God again. God knew all this, and loved him despite his faults and failures.

While King David received forgiveness from God, he also lost the son born because of his adultery. If when we sin—when we miss the bull's-eye—we abhor what we have done (or not done), we can be forgiven and restored to a right relationship with God yet still have a price to pay.

Think of it this way: if you put your hand in the fire, it will burn you. You may learn your lesson from it and sincerely determine never to do such a thing again, but the damage has already been done. It will take time for your hand to heal. In other words, it is going to hurt for a while. The same is true for the things we do that go against God's will. We may get burned and repent, but we still need time to heal.

This does not excuse our failures, but it should encourage us if think we must be perfect before God can accept us. He loves us even with our faults and failures. While God certainly calls Christians to a higher standard, this does not mean that we never fall. The difference is in whether or not we admit our fault, get up and press on. The one who falls and remains there, living a life of habitual sin, is the one who has a serious problem. Other than total rejection of God, there is no sin too big or too great for God to forgive. In our own weakness, we might have issues with an offender, but God is quick to forgive and forget. What a wonderful world it would be if we were all that way.

The injustices I have endured pale in comparison to those of many others. You may be going through far worse places. Consider the first century Christians unjustly persecuted to the point of death for their faith in Jesus Christ. Today injustice continues in a wide array. Christians are still persecuted, imprisoned and even killed for their confession of faith in God. Many must cope with the merciless and hurtful dealings of peers or other hateful people.

For example, it is common in schools today for some children to mercilessly taunt or bully their peers because they dress differently, or look different, or any of a host of meaningless criteria. Wars have raged for hundreds of years between the Catholics and Protestants, Christians and Muslims, and so on. In the wake of 9/11 there was a horrid backlash against anyone who was Muslim. Segregation used to be law in many states. Some African Americans today still hate Caucasians, and vice versa. Where I currently live there is a lot of distrust and dislike of Latinos, and I am sure the opposite is true as well. The Democrats and the Republicans cannot seem to get along, and so partisan politics reigns in our capital. Law enforcement often uses profiling, with the result that they sometimes arrest innocent people. There is religious injustice, political injustice, racial injustice and criminal injustice almost everywhere we look.

I have acknowledged my failures before God, and had to live with the consequences. I have done things in my life of which I am not proud, and like David even though forgiven have had to pay the price. While I do not like reaping the results of my sinful actions, I accept the need for correction and paying a penalty. Odd as it may sound, I am thankful for God's correction. To me it is one more way he proves his love for me. If he did not love me, he would not correct me.

There have been many instances of injustice in my life, but the one that stands out preeminently in my mind was ironically at the hands of the justice system. It was both a case of injustice, and of learning to forgive when wronged. I was unjustly charged with felony crimes, arrested, arraigned, jailed, indicted and later put on probation. One witness lied under oath about me, and I had to just sit there and take it for fear of angering the judge. I never pled guilty to the charges and never stood trial. I did, however, spend the better part of a year in and out of court, a lot of money in legal fees and a year and a half on probation for nothing more than a minor traffic accident.

For both my family and me it was a living nightmare. I cannot even begin to explain how dark a time it was and how crushing it felt. And yet I should not have been surprised.

Jesus told us that we would have tribulations, trials, distress and frustrations. Thankfully, he followed that seemingly depressing statement with one of hope, exhorting us to take courage because he has overcome the world and deprived it of power to harm us.[11] For me it was almost impossible to see that while in the thick of legal problems, and yet as I went through my nerve-wracking experience with the justice system God's word repeatedly came to me. His assurance and his promises not only comforted me, they helped me to stay at peace, trusting in him.

He repeatedly encouraged me, saying, "Do not be afraid. I am with you. I will strengthen and harden you to the trial. I will help you. I will hold you up.[12] I could go on at length about this fiasco, but God has led me to the place of forgiving those who meant me harm. That means putting it all behind me and seeking his blessing for them. You too can come through your trial victoriously.

My predicament did not even come close to the levels of injustice others have endured and today continue to endure. Consider the young woman who gives her heart to a man, only to have it broken after he gets her pregnant and decides he is not ready to take responsibility for the consequences of their actions, leaving her to raise their child alone.

Think about people in other nations who have no justice. Can you imagine what life is like under the Taliban? Is it acceptable to make it illegal for women to receive an education? Is it just to kill a woman because she does not wear a burqa out in public, and to then dump her body on garbage heaps as a warning to other women? What about life in China? There it is against the law for a husband and wife to have more than one child. If you have a second child, the government severely punishes you. And what about the innocent infants? Parents often kill female babies because they want a son to carry on the family name. They also abandon sickly male babies, leaving them to die.

Consider the woman who pours her heart and soul into her family, giving decades of her life to raising children, nurturing and teaching them, taking care of the home, doing the laundry, cooking meals, washing dishes and clothes, scrubbing floors and toilets, ironing, tending to sick children or a sick husband—all without so much as even an occasional thank you. Then, as if that is not enough, her husband abandons her because he has a "mid-life crisis," decides in his foolishness that there is no longer any value to their marriage and leaves her for another woman (usually younger). Consider the opposite, in which a couple divorces and one of them puts the other through a living hell, denying him or her the ability even to be a meaningful part of their children's lives.

We can all come up with a mile-long list of injustices. The point is, that while it may be our natural tendency to dwell on personal injustices and to become angry and bitter about such events, it is not God's desire for us to do so. He wants the very best for us. So why then does he allow us to go through all the garbage of life's injustices? Perhaps it would do us good to look at this whole issue from a different perspective.

An unknown author once said to another person, "Sometimes I would like to ask God why he allows poverty, suffering and injustice when he could do something about it."

The other's response was, "Well, why don't you ask him?"

"Because I'm afraid he would ask me the same question."

God will hold each of us accountable for what we do, and just as properly, for what we fail to do. We are commanded—not merely suggested—to feed the hungry, to visit those in prison and to take care of the poor, the orphans and widows.[13] How many of us are actually doing any of that? Jesus did not hold back or come up with excuses when he saw the need around him. He acted in ways that showed compassion by genuinely helping those in need.

We would have a lot less suffering and injustice in this world if we did what Jesus commanded us to do. Don't you think so? Instead, many of us sit and complain about unimportant things like how slow our "high speed" Internet connection is when there are people in our own communities who are sitting in the dark, people who have lost their jobs and do not know from where the next meal will come, people who fear they will not have heat in the winter, or who call a freeway underpass home because they have nowhere else to go. I say "we" because I am just as guilty of turning a blind eye to the needy, or of convincing myself that what I want to do at the time is more important than obeying Christ's command to help them. "Because I'm afraid he would ask me the same question" makes me stop in my tracks and brings to my remembrance the words of Christ when he said that when we have done these things to the most insignificant ones we have done it to him.[14]

What this all comes down to is that, while we have the right to ask God why there is evil and why injustice continues to happen, we do not have the right to judge God—especially when we have not stepped out of our selfishness to ask what we have done to help. What have we done? Good intentions do not count. In the end, we will each answer individually to God, and his questions and response will be perfectly just.

My God is not flighty or whimsical. He is the same today as he was when he formed the earth; and he will be the same millions, even billions of years from now. He tells us repeatedly that he cares for us, that he desires the best for us. Listen to these promise of his to you, "For the Lord your God is a merciful God; he will not fail you or destroy you or forget the covenant of your fathers, which he swore to them" (Deuteronomy 4:31).[15] He will not fail you. He will not destroy you. He will keep his promise to you.

Jesus made one of my dearest promises when he said he would be with us all the time—every minute of every day—through every trial and test.[16] In other words, no matter what I am going through, Jesus is there with me. He is my constant companion, my most devoted friend, the one who never gives up on me and who is always there to whisper words of hope, encouragement and love.

I have suffered much in my life. Others have suffered even more. Perhaps you have too. I sympathize. No, I empathize. Some of the injustices I have had to endure seemed impossible at the time. They were painful. They lasted far longer than I thought I could endure them. Yet they have taught me much about life, faith, character, mercy and forgiveness. While I do not long to suffer injustice of any kind, I am encouraged that God will always go through those places with me, that he allows them for his greater purpose, and that his desire is for my best, for your best, regardless of what we see in the moment. Every trial, every injustice, every test, every failure of mine is another episode of being chiseled and formed into what God sees in and purposes for me. He will do the same for you if you will let him.

Chiseled by Trial

FAKE IT 'TIL YOU MAKE IT

Jesus knows me. This I love.

Unknown

The three years that I worked for a company that facilitated marketing research were quite a revelation for me. I had the questionable privilege of witnessing some behaviors I did not expect from professionals, but then perhaps I was just naïve. Because it helped me to face some of my own faults, it was good for me. Some of it was not so good, and some of it just left me scratching my head in wonder.

The firm's technology department consisted of, well, me. As the resident "alpha-geek" (the one with the most technical abilities), I was accustomed to being called on to resolve issues with computer systems that ranged from trivial to major. Most often the issue would be something minor and easily remedied—provided one knew what to do to fix it. We in the trade joke about ID-10-T and PEBCAK errors. ID-10-T is simply "idiot." PEBCAK is an acronym for "problem exists between chair and keyboard," meaning the person, not the computer, was the problem.

Often the call would begin with an apologetic "I'm so sorry to call you, and I know this is probably a stupid question, but ..."

I eventually got to the point of trying to ease the caller's state of embarrassment by saying, "There are no stupid questions, but there are a lot of inquisitive idiots." That usually got a laugh and let the caller know I was not the stereotypical technician with an obvious chip on his shoulder.

Occasionally the person calling had reached the limit of his/her patience with a computer and belligerently barked out their complaints, taking their frustrations out on me. As I said, I was used to it, so the calls were often opportunities to leave my desk for a few minutes and make someone else feel better by fixing their problem.

If you work in marketing research, it is not my intent here to offend you. Marketing researchers are often a breed apart, and that is not a compliment. Many of them are wonderful people. I met some who just blessed me beyond expectation. Several of them, however, managed to leave a bad taste in my mouth. Is that just my near-sighted and skewed perception? Perhaps. One of my weakest areas is in dealing with people who seem to think they are better than everyone else. I am equally sure that I left some of them upset with me.

When this sort would come to our facility to conduct their research, they expected the royal treatment. No joke. They really expected to be treated like kings and queens. On later reflection, I think I understand why they acted that way. When they are at home with their parent companies, they are on the bottom of the food chain. When they leave their home office to go to a research facility, it is their opportunity to be on the top. They are on the road a lot, and work very strange and tiring hours. Regardless of what motivated them, they expected a lot! We had one staff member whose sole responsibility was literally to cater to their every desire. Whatever they wanted to eat or drink she provided with a smile.

One day a researcher demanded—not asked, demanded—for the caterer to run out to the grocery store and bring back three different kinds of bananas. It did not matter that there were bananas in the suite already. This woman wanted to see three specific kinds of bananas from which to make her selection. In the larger picture, that is not a big deal. I do, however, think it reveals something important about the character of the person making the demand.

Anyway, when the caterer returned with the bananas, the woman barked out, "Peel that one for me." That was a bit rude, but the caterer just smiled and peeled the banana onto a plate for her. In the next heartbeat the researcher snarled, "Slice if up for me." If I had been the caterer, I more than likely would have turned and left Ms. Queen Bee to slice it up herself. I know that would not be a good reflection of Christ, but I get that way sometimes. The caterer just smiled, cut the banana up for her, keeping the customer happy. Well, as happy as *she* could be.

Later, I asked the caterer why she put up with that kind of treatment. We had a short conversation about it which, as I was getting back on the elevator to return to my office, ended with her advice to me, "Fake it 'til you make it!" Naturally, her advice came with a huge smile.

Her philosophy—as well meaning as it was for client satisfaction—was to pretend to enjoy what she was doing with the hope that one day either she would change so that all the unrealistic demands no longer bother her, or until her ship comes in and she does not have to pretend any more. In other words, be a phony until either you change or the situation changes. Sorry, I dislike pretending, and would rather swim out than wait for my ship to come in.

While I have had extensive theological training, I prefer to think of myself as a pragmatist, so this "fake it 'til you make it" philosophy puzzled me. I did a little research on it for my own satisfaction. The phrase originated as the title of a book by Phil Kerns in his expose of Amway when he left that company.

Now, there *are* times when we must simply grin and bear it. There are many times every day when we have to just press through and do something we would rather not; but, come on, let us be honest with each other. At some point we have pretty much all worked at jobs we disliked a lot. If I did not understand that we often have to do things we do not feel like doing, well I cannot tell you how many times I would not have gone to work or would have left in the middle of the day. The Bible tells us that whatever we do we should do it as if we are doing it for the Lord.

A more common interpretation of this fake it 'til you make it phrase is that you should pretend to exude confidence in your own abilities even when you feel incapable. The idea there is that if you do this enough, the pretend success created in your own mind will in turn produce true confidence. What a load of psychobabble.

The purpose of all this fakery is to avoid getting stuck in a self-fulfilling prophecy about one's fears and lack of confidence. Should we really keep going through life as if we are enjoying everything about it even though it feels forced? If you follow this philosophy, they say, eventually you will become confident. I am just not one of those people who can go around pretending to be happy, successful, and confident when the reality is that my life is going downhill in a hurry. It is when I am in those very places that I need help and prayer, not acclaim from others for being good at living a lie.

Pop psychology, like the fake it 'til you make it crowd, is rarely—if ever—on target. No matter how well disguised this philosophy may be, it is nothing more than an approach of mind over matter. A better description might be wishful thinking. Think of it as an etch-a-sketch instead of a painting. I once had a watch that had written on its face "Novado." I think my wife paid $10 for it. It was a knock-off, a fake. No matter how much I may have tried to pass it off as the real McCoy, it was still a phony.

If this is your approach to dealing with problems or trying to get ahead, then I have a few questions for you. How well is that working for you? Are you happy? Have you overcome? Have your dreams come true? Probably not, at least not to the degree you might desire. You are faking it, and you know that you are faking it. You are wasting your time trying to pretend and knowing you are pretending.

Instead of pretending, use that same time and energy with God's leading in order to make the changes in your life that need to happen. Does it really make any sense to waste your time and energy on something that is not real? Not to me!

Here is where it breaks down. Because you know you are faking it, the very act of faking it constantly reminds you that you have not made it. Think about that for a minute. Allow it to sink in. That is simply how our brains work. The more you fake it the more you feel like an imposter because—like it or not—that is exactly what you are.

Here is the truth. We all have strengths and weaknesses. What I am good at others are not good at, and in what others are good at I am woefully lacking. As unique individuals, God does not mean for us to take something that seems impossible or unnatural and pretend it is the easiest most natural thing in the world. For example, I can barely draw stick figures much less something that even closely resembles art. Even if I wanted to be an artist, I am not going to pretend that art is the most natural, easiest thing in the world for me because it is not; and doing so would be a lie. It does not matter how hard I try, or how much I pretend to exude confidence in my artistic abilities. It just is not in my makeup.

On the other hand, drawing and painting seem to come as easy as breathing to at least three of my four children, but none of them can find their way around computer network security the way I can. We have different natural tendencies, interests and gifts, so why pretend to be something we are not? Instead, focus your time and energy on the gifts and talents with which God has blessed you.

Many Christians misinterpret a passage in Proverbs that they think speaks about raising children in the Christian faith (and we should raise our children with knowledge of our faith and of God). The passage in the King James Version says, "Train up a child in the way he should go: and when he is old, he will not depart from it" (Proverbs 22:6). They interpret the phrase "the way he should go" to mean the ways of God and in particular of Christian faith. I disagree. It more accurately means "in keeping with his or her individual gift or bent."[1] Bible commentator Albert Barnes says this phrase means "the path especially belonging to, especially fitted for, the individual's character. The proverb enjoins the closest possibly study of each child's temperament and the adaption of 'his way of life' to that." Therefore, we ought to teach each other to be who we are as God created us rather than pretending to be what we are not.

If we try to use this fake it 'til you make it philosophy, we will wind up confused, depressed and the victims of our own attempts. The fake it 'til you make it evangelists preach the use of your will power to overcome your natural habits until they have changed. While we do need to be willful in our thoughts and actions where and when appropriate, this philosophy of life is simply wrong because it fails to take into account that it goes against the entire design of your brain and body. What these promoters refuse to see is that fake it 'til you make it is a painful and often damaging way to try to change your life. God just did not make your brain to work that way.

That does not mean we should never attempt anything that does not come easily or naturally. Concert grade musicians are not born able to play beautifully. They consistently practice. They do have a natural predisposition that attracts them to their music and in which if they work hard at it, they can excel. The same is true for any skill—music, art, writing, debate, raising children, mathematics, chemistry, medicine, and so on. I think God frequently stretches those of us who earnestly want to him to use us. He stretches us outside of our comfort zones, and the result is wonderful because we are his handiwork. It is one thing, however, to allow him to stretch you, and it is another to keep at something that just is not going to work for you because it is not in your makeup.

Most of us have seen the motivational posters that so many businesses put up in their offices about customer support, teamwork, and so on. I still grin whenever I recall the "de-motivational" poster that says, "Quitters never win, winners never quit, but those who never win AND never quit are idiots."[2] That is how I see the fake it 'til you make it philosophy. Hopelessly chasing after something that is beyond my abilities is a futile effort and a colossal waste of time and energy.

So what then is the answer to the dilemma? I suggest that we need to get in touch with the unique combination of natural abilities and spiritual gifts with which God has uniquely blessed each of us, and to look to him to bring about whatever change he desires to see in us instead of trying to manipulate him into going along with our myopic desires. If we seek his will in our lives rather than our own, he will equip us to do more than we can dream.

The psalmists often use the phrase "my walk," and what that means is our day-in, day-out lifestyle. It is the little things—the habits that make up our way of living. Do we do the things that God desires of us, that bring his blessings and favor; or do we do the things that we prefer over what we know he expects from us?

Allow me to give you an example. Last year I was heavier than I am today, and the reason I was overweight was that I ate and drank more than I should. My eating and drinking habits caused me to reap the harvest of thirty pounds of body fat. For a time I tried to ignore it by pretending I was not really overweight. I just had a little "middle aged spread." That was faking it, and it sure was not taking me in the right direction. It also was not fooling anyone—not even me. So I changed my habits. I started exercising regularly, eating and drinking less and taking in more water than dehydrating beverages like coffee. This lifestyle change—over the course of a year—resulted in my losing that unwanted and unhealthy weight. It took commitment and diligence. It did not come easy or quickly, but the change did come progressively. I faced reality rather than faking it.

Our habits, our way of life, our walk will lead us in either the right direction or the wrong direction. If our habits do not include taking time regularly to draw close to

God and to seek his leading, then more than likely we are walking down the wrong path. The habits that bring success and satisfaction are both those that God has naturally gifted us with, and those to which he points us.

For example, I have natural abilities with analysis, comprehension and organization. These abilities make it easier for me to study Scripture than it does for many others. On the other hand, God often has to prod me to spend more time digging deeper into his Word. As much as I enjoy mining Scripture, I often would prefer to read a novel or watch a movie—usually something that does not involve much mental effort. Therefore, I need to cultivate the habit of spending time in prayer and in Bible reading and study. That is not faking it. It is actively taking the steps I need to in order to reach the goal of being closer— and remaining close—to God.

While our emotions should not rule our conduct, neither should we ignore them. I think we would all do well to take on the ancient Hebrew view of man: each of us is a whole package. We are not three separate compartments of physical body, logical mind and emotions. Body, mind and heart are all a part of the whole person. Sometimes we do have to just grit our teeth and determine to be happy in the middle of a crisis, or confident or comfortable with a specific situation for a time, but not as a habit or what runs cross grain to our God-given nature.

It is true that we sometimes must to do things we do not feel like doing. This is not the same as acting as if something is true when it is false. I may not desire to work on a given task, but it may be precisely what God wants me to be doing. How I choose to perceive any given situation plays a big part in how it actually affects me. For example, if a customer decides to get ugly and pushy with me, how do I respond? Should I pretend that I am okay with their abusive language or behavior? I have to deal with it—put up with it even—but I do not have to pretend that it is okay or that it does not affect me.

As one who tries to allow the Holy Spirit to lead me, I can choose to take the high road and be gracious to an abusive person because that is how God deals with me. After all, I am supposed to do everything as if I am doing it directly for him. I can pray for wisdom in dealing with an upset customer as well as praying for them to see how their behavior affects others. Moreover, with God's help I can do that without being abusive back to them or becoming stressed about it. Choosing to seek God's leading can become a habit—a lifestyle—that helps me to be a better person who also reflects God better because I submit to his will rather than trying to get others to bend to mine.

What we have to learn is to humble ourselves and do with all our might whatever it is God has given us to do. That does not come easily or naturally for most of us because our faith walk is not an easy one. God did not promise us an easy life. In fact, as I have already stated, Jesus cautioned us that we would have trials and tests. The Christian's walk, however difficult it may be at times, is a blessed life.

We also need to realize that what matters is not how we think of ourselves, but rather how God thinks of us. There is a big difference there. I am sure that if we could ask any of the heroes of the Bible what they thought of themselves none of them would say he or she was a person of great faith or that they had lived a faultless life before God. And yet God said of Caleb, that he "followed me fully," and he referred to Job as "a perfect and an upright man."[3]

At the conclusion of his address to Christians in Colossae, and immediately following his instructions to slaves, Paul told them to avoid trying to butter up others, to work from the heart for their real master, Jesus, knowing that in the end God will bless them with a heavenly inheritance.[4] To live as a Christian means to follow God persistently and consistently—not just now and then, but all your life. It does not mean you never slip up. It means you follow him sincerely—from the heart—not just with good intentions but also with all your heart, with every ounce of desire and energy. It means to follow him exclusively—not following pop-psychology, our own desires or anything or anyone else whenever and wherever they do not follow God. We are not to follow anyone— pastor, teacher, leader of any sort—any farther than he or she is following God.

None of this should lead to the conclusion that we are wise to fake it 'til we make it. What it does mean is that the attitude of our hearts should be that of a willing servant. When Paul wrote that he was "a servant of Christ," the word he used identified him as someone who voluntarily chose to remain a slave in his master's household.[5] Being a servant in a godly sense does not come from coercion or force. It comes instead out of love for the one served.

So how do we get to the point of being able to have the right attitude about doing the things we do not like doing? A few of us are strong enough to force ourselves, but even those have their moments. The answer of course is that we cannot get there on our own. We have to—here it comes again—die to self. It is "Christ within and among you, the Hope of [realizing the] glory,"[6] who enables us to become willing servants. Then we are not faking it. Then we are indeed making it ... in Christ.

Chiseled by Trial

FEELING WORTHLESS

Feelings of worthlessness are as common,
and fall into the same category as headaches—
they're all in your head.

One of the oddities of life is that as talented, gifted or needed any one of us may be, at some point in our life we all feel worthless. I do not know about you, but I can feel alone, separated and without any redeeming value even when I am at home surrounded by my family who love me. My biggest personal battle has always been with self-worth.

One of my dear friends once referred to me as an overachiever because throughout graduate school I usually got near-perfect scores on my final exams. My point is not that I am some super-smart person, but that while I have good reason to be self-confident, instead I often feel like a miserable failure, that I just do not cut it. I have achieved many things in my lifetime—some rewarded, and others unnoticed.

The United States Air Force awarded me the Air Force Achievement Medal for manually deciphering a long and important encoded radio message in the field. It was not anything monumental in my eyes. It was—as most military people think of their actions—a case of simply doing my job. On another occasion, I spent hours out in the hot and steamy summer afternoon sun, voluntarily directing traffic around a major accident on the Massachusetts State Pike. As if I was personally responsible for their inconvenience, several ungrateful drivers swore at me. A few months after this incident the Air Force decorated another man in my unit who simply drove a wrecker to get the truck out of the highway median. Nobody ever said so much as a thank you to me. I felt a little bit disappointed about that, but in the grander scheme of things, it really did not matter.

Of far greater significance to me is that I have successfully raised four children into mature, socially responsible—and for the most part well-adapted—adults who are doing their part to contribute to the betterment of society. That alone is something for which to be grateful. Adding to what should be a feeling of worth; I served in the United States Air Force for 24 years, from the Vietnam War through the first Gulf War. I have achieved recognition from employers, the military and individuals. I have earned prestigious degrees in higher education. I have made a positive impact on the lives of at least a few people. So why then do I so often feel like a total failure?

Why is it that when everything is going well I get depressed and fear that I am just not cutting it? Why do I so often think I have failed my family, my employer, my friends, my fellow Christians and my God? I know I am not alone in feeling this way. Many of us have doubts that frequently nag at us about our abilities, our motivation and our value as human beings. Because we can be prone to exaggerated self-perceptions, now and then it can be a good thing to step back and take stock of what we are doing and why. In other words, our easily inflated egos can benefit from an occasional reality check to help us avoid getting bigheaded. However, in the past the occasional self-test was not my normal mode of thinking.

Occasionally I get unjustifiably proud, and then God quickly gets me by in line by sending someone along to burst my bubble. More often, however, the way I think of myself is that I am not good enough: I am not good enough at my job, I do not know enough to do it as well as others; I am not good enough as a father, a husband, a pastor, a student, a writer, a technician, and so on. To me, it does not seem to matter how much I know or do or how hard I may work at it. I am just not good enough. A lot of the time, I feel that I am lacking in what really is important.

For reasons I often fail to understand, feeling worthless is one of my weakest areas. I struggle constantly with this because, more often than not I am keenly aware of my failures and shortcomings. I do not know why I tend to focus on those instead of what God thinks of me. I am well educated. I live in a nice house on a delightful corner lot in a lovely, quiet and a friendly town. I have a good job, and my peers respect me. When I teach, people often tell me that I am a gifted teacher.

So why do I so often feel ashamed of myself? It is, quite simply, because I know how often I *do* fail, which is every day. Even if nobody else knows, God knows. I also know the secrets about myself that most never see. It embarrasses me to say that I can drive to work and praise God's handiwork in front of me with one breath, and with the next become angry when someone cuts me off in traffic and say things that should not come out of my mouth. Why is it that I so easily raise my voice or speak sarcastically to those I love when I should instead speak to them quietly and peacefully, encouraging and building them up?

It should not come as a surprise that, like everyone else, I have done things of which I am ashamed. I have lied. It does not matter how small or large the lie may have been, that makes me a liar. We are all liars because each of us has at least once told a lie. I have taken things that were not mine. It does not matter if it was just a paper clip or someone's car. That makes me a thief. We are all thieves. At some point, every one of us has taken something that was not ours—even if it was nothing more than snatching a cookie when mom was not looking. I have tried to deceive people. I have gossiped about others. I have dishonored my wife. I have told coarse jokes. I have gotten drunk and— worse—I turned my back on God and walked away from him. Thankfully, he never let go of me and, eventually like the Prodigal's son, I came back to him.

In spite of all that, I am in good company. Even the apostle Paul made the same kind of complaints about his own behavior.[1] He confessed that whenever he decided to do what was good, he failed. When he decided not to do bad things, he would go ahead and do them anyway. He often felt helpless. Does that strike a chord in you? I bet it does. It is our flesh, our sin nature; or as many like to say in churches, it is the "old man" in each of us.

Even though I know the source of these feelings, I still must often battle with them. Rare is the person in Christian circles today who is unfamiliar with the term Satan. He is not some whacked out person in a red suit with horns, a tail and a pitchfork. Have you ever stopped to think about the meaning of his name? Etymology—the study of the history of words—might bore you to tears, but it fascinates me. By examining the history of the words we use we can gain insights into our culture. Case in point: The word Satan means "the accuser." The word in Hebrew literally means "adversary"[2]—one opposed to us, an enemy who stands and slings accusations at us. This is significant. It is precisely what Satan does.[3] He stands and accuses us before God. If you have ever watched any of the court television shows, then you will have no trouble identifying an accuser, an adversary.

With that in mind, it should not come as a surprise that any of us feels worthless now and then. These feelings of worthlessness are simply one of the attacks of our adversary, our accuser; and all too often are quite effective. "You're worthless. You failed … again. You can't cut it. You'll never amount to anything. What an idiot you are. Who are you trying to fool? You know you're worthless. You're ugly. My goodness, you've gotten fat. You'll never amount to anything." On and on his litany goes, driving us down, down, down. Why would he want to do that? It is not because he is mean and does not like you or that he wants to make your life miserable. He attacks your feelings of self-worth because he hates the one who created you, the

God of whom you are a reflection. He levels his attack not against you in particular but rather against God.

As I was thinking about these issues one day, and wondering why I feel these ways about past—and sometimes present behaviors—the Holy Spirit brought a passage of the apostle John's fist epistle before my eyes, and the words jumped off the page. (I love when that happens.) Writing to his "dear children," John said, "… if our heart accuses us, God is greater than our heart and knows all things. Beloved, if our heart does not accuse us, we have confidence toward God."[4]

At first, the second part of that passage appeared to dash all hope for me of ever being free from this condemning heart of mine, but a deeper examination of it gave me hope. I especially like the way The Message translates this passage. Keep in mind that The Message is not a literal translation. It is a paraphrase meant to convey the ideas in an easily understood manner. In that paraphrase John writes, "It's also the way to shut down debilitating self-criticism, even when there is something to it. For God is greater than our worried hearts and knows more about us than we do ourselves. And friends, once that is taken care of and we're no longer accusing or condemning ourselves, we're bold and free before God."

Noted leader of the worldwide evangelical movement in the late 1960s and early 1970s, and author of the now classic Christian book, "Basic Christianity," John R. W. Stott, says of this passage of scripture,

It is within the general context of the letter's teaching on assurance that this paragraph about the condemning heart must be read. However firmly grounded the Christian's assurance is his heart may sometimes need reassurance. Indeed ... the first phrase of verse 20 "whenever our hearts condemn us," the suggestion seems to be that it may not be either an unusual or an infrequent experience for the Christian's serene assurance to be disturbed. Sometimes the accusations of our "conscience" ... will be true accusations, and sometimes they will be false, inspired by "the accuser of our brothers" ... In either case, the inner voice is not to overcome us. We are rather to set our hearts at rest in his presence, that is, we must be able to do so in the sight of God (the words in his presence are emphatic)."[5]

Did you catch that? The apostle was writing to Christians. He was writing to them about assurance and love. Therefore, the Christians to whom he was writing must have shown some anxieties about their standing with God because of their imperfections. The lesson here is that we *are* imperfect and always will be in this life. By our own striving, we will never measure up to God's standards. We cannot. The good news is that we do not have to. Stott goes on to say that, "It is implied that we shall be able to do this only if we know that we belong to the truth." If that is the case, it begs the question, "how can we know?" To get the answer we must first do what is called for in any good study of scripture—look first at the context of the particular passage.

Leading up to those two verses, John had been writing about love, of not being hypocrites saying we love one another yet stabbing each other in the back, being jealous, gossiping, and so on. We all know what I am talking about. Much to our discredit, the Church is often full of people who say one thing and do another. John did not beat around the bush on that matter. He called them liars. He said the truth is not in them. Ouch!

The love John wrote of is not some namby-pamby emotionalism. As Stott puts it, "not things we have professed, or felt or imagined or intended, but things we have done ... If we thus love 'in truth,' we may indeed have full assurance in our hearts. 'The fruit of love is confidence.'" It is this kind of real love that shows itself in actions (see 1 Corinthians chapter 13 for a great list of love in action). Love is far more than mere emotion. It is more importantly what we *do*, how we act toward each other.

If you read John's fist epistle—his first letter to the Church—you will find in the third chapter two tests of a true child of God. These two tests reveal whether or not how we live lines up with what we say. Are we walking the walk or just talking the talk? The two evidences of indeed being a Christian are that, as Dr. Ian A. H. Bond, Vice-President of Beacon Seminary said, "You will take after your Father. You will take to your brother."[6] In other words, your character and behavior will reflect that of God, and you will love in actions your fellow Christians. If these things are not true of us then we simply are not children of

God. If we are children of God—if his "seed" is in us—then it is inevitable that we will become more and more like him.[7]

A grass seed cannot become a tree. It will reflect the grass from which it came by growing into the same kind of grass. An apple seed will never become a banana tree. It will grow into an apple tree that is a reflection of its source. Likewise, if God's seed is in us then we will be a reflection of him as we grow.

While most of us understand what it means to love our brother—our neighbor, our co-worker, our fellow human beings—many have difficulty wrapping their minds around what it means to "take after" our heavenly Father. John says we are to have confidence before God. My question was, "How do we get to that point?" Once again, we cannot on our own. In our religious mindsets, many of us seem to feel we can never be pure enough to stand confidently before such a holy God, or that even thinking we can is being flippant or irreverent in our attitude toward him. And yet the writer of Hebrews exhorts us to come boldly—with confidence—in order to obtain God's grace.[8]

The tendency to think we can never be holy enough to come before God (much less to come boldly) is grounded in two things. First, in ourselves, we *are* unworthy, and most of us know this to be true. Whether or not we are willing to admit it is another matter. Second, it is not because of our own strength, holiness, or anything else within our own being that we are able to come before God at all. It is only because of the work of the Son of God, Jesus Christ. That is why I can stand before God like a child before his loving father and call out to him boldly and without irreverence, "Daddy!"

It is my prayer that no one reading this book will ever have to face a judge in court. It is an extremely uncomfortable feeling. When you stand before a judge you are quite literally there to be judged. There will be a pronouncement of guilt or innocence. If judged guilty then there will be a sentencing—a fine, jail time, or some combination. Somebody is going to pay. Occasionally a judge will extend mercy—or as we call it today, leniency—to someone he or she convicts. A person caught driving without a license will receive a fine and maybe time in jail. A person who robs a store at gunpoint will rightfully receive a more severe judgment—most likely years in prison. Imagine the awful feeling of standing before the God of the universe where the punishment is eternal torment (in my opinion, separation from God). None of us—not even one—has ever or will ever be righteous enough to stand before God on our own and not expect to be condemned. In our own righteousness, we are all guilty.

There was a time when I owed a couple thousand dollars to a credit card company, and because of my own failures, I had not paid them on time or in accordance with the contract. The company hired a lawyer to have a lien put on my house. That meant that before title to the house could pass to anyone else; I would have to repay the entire amount owed plus the attorney's fees, plus interest, late fees, and so on. When I had to stand before the judge, I felt miserable and utterly helpless. I had no one there to help me. I did not know the system. I did not know what could or could not be done, and was at the mercy of a lawyer who knew the system well. For him it was child's play, and I think he enjoyed watching me squirm. I would have felt much better if I had had someone there to speak for me, who knew the law, who knew all the options and what to say. I was guilty, and I did not have a lawyer to speak for me. Well, when it comes to facing God we have such an attorney. Jesus Christ stands before him on our behalf, and when we are accused he says, "Yes, he's guilty, but I have already paid his debt in full."

So, let us get back to how we can be confident. John says that we can know we are God's and can "reassure (quiet, conciliate, and pacify) our hearts in his presence."[9] In other words, we do not have to fear standing before the Judge, and here is where the light bulb went on for me: this confidence is not self-confidence. It is not arrogance or wishful thinking. As Dr. Ian A. H. Bond said, "A Christian may be terribly unsure about himself, but he has confidence before God."[10] Now here is the blessed hope for my poor harried heart. An unbeliever does not have a heart that condemns him. It is the Christian whose heart condemns him or her because God has awakened your conscience. We feel condemned because we have a conscience that is no longer dead to God.

What did God say to my frustrated and self-condemning heart? He said, "Why are you condemning yourself? I knew the worst about you before I accepted you." As with Peter's pride at being Jewish and unwilling to eat food that was not Kosher, God was warning me to not turn my nose up at what he has already approved—even at myself.

So what is the deal about feeling condemned and unworthy of anyone much less of God? Often our conscience justly accuses us. Writing of our condemning hearts, highly regarded Bible scholar F.F. Bruce said that at such times "only when it is overruled by the pardoning edict of God can its voice be properly hushed."[11] Just picture your heart standing up and shouting, "Objection!" and God smacking his hammer and declaring, "Overruled!"

Where I am going with this is that we have an accuser who will use every trick in the book to make us feel like failures so we will give up and live defeated; but if we confess our sins, we can live in peace with hearts that do not condemn us.

One of the keys here is what constitutes our habitual behavior. Do we occasionally slip up, or is that our normal lifestyle? If it is the former, then we are okay—provided we confess when we do fail. If it is the latter, then we need to get a healthy fear of God into our lives so that we do not live a lifestyle of habitual sin. I have often slipped and done minor things like swearing. I even failed in a big way decades ago when I broke my vows to my wife. I should not do either, but neither is my day-to-day behavior. When I fail, I feel bad about it, confess my failure to God and seek his forgiveness. I go beyond just being sorry: I try not to repeat it. If either extreme becomes my normal behavior, then I have a bigger problem.

Even then, God can and will forgive us if we sincerely renounce such behavior and seek to live as we know we should. The alcoholic, the drug addict, the one who cannot stay away from pornography, the thief, the adulterer, and so on—none of us is beyond God's reach to forgive and to restore. What a blessed hope!

Finally, it is not something we will ever accomplish by our own strength. It is all the work of Jesus Christ—and only because of his work—that it is possible for us to come before God confident and without condemnation.

Stott further clarifies this whole matter by stating, "The emphatic purpose of the whole paragraph is to heal the wounded conscience, not to open its wound wider, 'to give assurance, and not to strike terror into their hearts.'"12 Oh, I love that! I do not know who came up with it, but someone put a twist to the childhood song "Jesus loves me, this I know" which just blesses me all the time now. They sang, "Jesus knows me, this I love."

Thankfully, because of God's loving whispers and the trials he has allowed in my life, I have come to the place where I accept myself as I am. Sure, I continue to try to be a better reflection of my Father, but I still slip up. The point is that I am okay with me. So is God. If someone does not like that, he can take it up with the Almighty.

So then, this is what I have learned about feeling worthless—and it just blesses my socks off. I am in good shape despite the sometimes frequent and other times infrequent condemning of my own heart. It is confidence and obedience to God that leads me into intimacy with him. That, dear ones, is paramount. These are what have made it possible for me to hear God's voice in the recesses of my heart, in the storms of life, when the testing and the trials come. It is there—leaning into God, trusting in his promises; and resting on the assurance, with confidence in him—that he speaks his words of life and love into my heart—a heart that he loves and with which he desires to be more entwined than I can ever comprehend. That is my God. He just blows my mind!

STINKING THINKING

It is the nature of thought to find its way into action.

Christian Nevell Bovee[1]

It is said that we spend 98% of our time thinking about what is wrong, about our problems, about what might go wrong, about what we think is sure to go wrong and even about other people's problems. That is "stinking thinking."[2]

Allow me to give you a personal example. I came home from work one day. It had been a particularly difficult day for me on the job, and so I had a heavy workout at the gym after in order to unwind. By then I was really worn out. When I arrived home no one was there. I wanted to take a shower and simply relax for a few minutes out on our deck. I called my wife, and because she did not answer, I left a message for her about my immediate plans. Within a few minutes of getting out of the shower the phone rang. It was the office. There was a critical problem with one of our computers, and they needed my immediate help. I was on the phone for the next hour providing technical support.

When I finally hung up there was a message on my phone. My wife was livid, and without getting the facts was convinced that I was selfishly indulging my wish to relax while she was over at her sister's with our oldest daughter helping them finish moving into a new house. Did she really think I could read her mind? That is one form of stinking thinking, and I am just as guilty of it as the rest of us.

Worry and frustration with others are not the only kinds of stinking thinking. Pride is another insidious mindset, as is defeatism. There are so many ways of thinking that many of us fall into so often without even being aware of it. All too often, many of us either consciously or unconsciously entertain such thinking.

Before I go any further, allow me to clarify one point: false humility is not the answer either. Max Lucado said, "The proper perspective of self is not to think less of yourself, but to think of yourself less."[3] Having a healthy self-image is important. It is not, however, the same thing as pride. Jesus told us to, "… love your neighbor as [you do] yourself."[4] Balance is important, but not the goal. Solomon warned us in Proverbs of the other side, saying that pride precedes destruction and our failure.[5] The great apostle Paul, writing from his deep affection for Christians in Philippi, instructed them about getting too proud or self-centered. He said:

"SO BY whatever [appeal to you there is in our mutual dwelling in Christ, by whatever] strengthening and consoling and encouraging [our relationship] in him [affords], by whatever persuasive incentive there is in love, by whatever participation in the [Holy] Spirit [we share], and by whatever depth of affection and compassionate sympathy … having the same love, being in full accord and of one harmonious mind and intention. Do nothing from factional motives [through contentiousness, strife, selfishness, or for unworthy ends] or prompted by conceit and empty arrogance. Instead, in the true spirit of humility (lowliness of mind) let each regard the others as better than and superior to himself [thinking more highly of one another than you do of yourselves.]"[6]

We should have a healthy image of ourselves. We are, after all, God's creation, made in his image. However, where some of us stray is that our view of ourselves has become distorted and out of proper perspective. We think of ourselves as being more important than others. In today's society the cry is "looking out for number one" or "it's all about me." That is the wrong perspective. It is a deadly view of self. A correct view of ourselves is necessary so that we will care more about others. We are not to become so enamored with ourselves that we think we are the center of the universe—because we are not. Our supreme example, Jesus Christ, is one of self-sacrifice. He was straightforward about it, saying, "Just as the Son of Man came not to be waited on but to serve, and to give his life as a ransom for many [the price paid to set them free]" (Matthew 20:28 AMP).

It was for us that even as the Son of God he humbled himself, became a human and in our place took the punishment we deserved. We have no right to get so full of ourselves that we do not even have the time of day for others. Our center, our proper balance, our focus is not to be on ourselves, but on sacrificially serving others in love and true concern for their welfare. When I say sacrificially, I mean that it costs you something. Giving sacrificially does not mean when it is convenient. More often it means when it is inconvenient.

Frequently I hear a form of this imbalance in complaints from people who are out "church hunting," or as I like to put it, "church shopping," looking for a church to call home but never quite finding what they want. They say, "Oh, yes. I've been to The-Church-of-(fill in the blank), but that place just didn't meet my needs." In other words, their main concern is "What's in it for me?" News alert: the primary purpose of church services is not to meet *your* needs.

Church services are not only meant for believers to worship and focus on God. They are also meant to prepare Christians to meet the needs of those living around them— outside the walls of the church. The end results of worship services are more for unbelievers than for fellow Christians. We are to meet the needs of the world. We are not called to be spiritual consumers. We are called to be participants, to get into the game, to reach out, to use the talents with which God has gifted us and to love those whom others have rejected—especially those who are not like us.

While we certainly do need to assemble together in order to build each other up, that is not the main reason for such gatherings. The primary purpose of church assemblies, and the gifts of service that God has given in different measures to each of us, is to "equip us for the work of the ministry."[7] The word "ministry" means service.[8] The better question, therefore, is to ask, "What can I be doing to help others?"

Jesus hung out with tax collectors, prostitutes, fishermen—those of whom the religious leaders then thought the least. Far too often, those of us who claim to represent Christ reject the ones who most need love. Jesus loves not only non-believers but also "second-class Christians" and even non-Christians. So should we.

When we know someone is in need, it is selfish to say, "I'll pray for you" when more often than not that is all we do—say we will pray. By all means do pray for those in need, but do not leave it there. Start by reaching out in practical ways to help meet their needs, and pray for them. Do you know of someone who needs groceries? Go out and buy some for them, or give them some of yours. Has their electricity been turned off? Help them to get it turned on again by digging into your pockets. Do you know of someone who has no home? Put them up for a while, and help them to get back on their feet—even if it means doing without.

Sacrificial love costs us something. It is not sacrificial if it is easy and costs us little or nothing. Sacrifice is giving up something in order to give to another. If you are not giving something up, then you are not sacrificing. If I have $100,000 in the bank (I wish!), and I buy someone a hamburger, that is not a sacrifice. If I have $200 in the bank and have wanted to get my car's air conditioner fixed, but instead use that money to help a widow on a fixed income with her utility bills, that is a sacrifice.

My family once helped a woman we knew was in need of real help. We considered up front what we thought it would cost us. We knew it would be an inconvenience to bring her into our home and have her sleep in our living room for a couple of weeks, but we could handle it—or so we thought. After all, that is what Jesus would have done. Sure, we would probably be a bit uncomfortable, but it would not be all that bad. It would stretch us a little, but it would not really be that big of a deal. The weeks turned into months. It became a strain on us rather than just a stretch.

We were learning firsthand about sacrifice. It turned out to be more than giving up a little space in the living room. We fed her and put a roof over her head for three months. She needed more than just food and a place to sleep. She needed emotional support, conversation, affirmation, social interaction, financial help, and to be driven around town when it did not easily fit into our schedules. It took its toll on nearly everything our family did for a quarter of a year. It became emotionally and economically draining. It cost us more than we had anticipated, but it was the right thing to do. It blessed her and as it turned out it also blessed us.

It was not all a bad experience. She tried to encourage us. She tried to be helpful, and, I have no doubt that she felt uncomfortable at times too. Do we regret having reached out to her in her time of need? Of course not. We knew it was what our Lord wanted us to do. It was being true to our calling as Christians to do more than merely profess our belief, and it became a good lesson for the two of our four children who were still living at home with us. They got a real-life look at what it means to love others, what it can cost and why it is needed.

Having said all of that, here is one area where many times I have fallen down. I have not consciously thought of myself as being better than everyone else. In fact, God's commands to love and honor others before myself have been so ingrained in my thinking that it disturbs me when someone appears selfish, arrogant or callous in his or her treatment of others. In fact, one of the quickest ways to irritate me is to come across as someone who thinks he is better than everyone else. I am not alone in that. God hates—not merely dislikes—he hates pride and arrogance.[9]

Most of us can easily think of examples: the man who thinks he deserves to cut around everyone else to the front of the line, the driver who feels justified in endangering the lives of others in order to get one or two car lengths ahead, the one who has to have a loud telephone conversation in a restaurant (or worse, in a public restroom), the person who walks directly across your path as if you were not even there (one of my pet peeves, which has become a standing joke between my wife and me), the one who seems to feel justified in racing into the parking place into which you were beginning to turn, even the kid with the blaring car stereo who has to cruise up and down your street late at night can appear self-centered when you are tired and just not in the mood for the noise.

For many years I felt justified in getting upset with people who behave those ways. Sometimes I still do. Then God's chisel struck again. What he said to me came as a mild shock. He said, "You are being more horrid in your thinking about these others than you think they are in their lack of thinking about you. You are being judgmental of them—which is not your job. I am judge, not you, so knock it off." Ouch. That smarted, and even more because it was the truth. It finally dawned on me that when I was thinking about how I did not like seeing what I perceived as arrogance or selfishness in others that I was actively judging them.

Because I was not acting the way they were (so I thought), I was subconsciously thinking I was better. What a delusion and both a clear case of flawed thinking and circular logic. I thought they were clearly in the wrong in their self-centeredness, but in thinking that way I was actually the one who was being self-centered, self-righteous and displeasing to God. What disturbed me most about this was the revelation that this mindset had crept in without a conscious decision on my part to be that way. I had unwittingly developed a mindset of stinking thinking.

Stinking thinking can be more than just how we think of others. All too often, many of us allow ourselves to be overly elated or discouraged because of what we assume about ourselves. (See the previous chapter.) Our faulty thinking can lead us to negative reactions about our problems, relationships or circumstances. Our irrational views often lead to destructive feelings and behavior. And here is the eye-opener: we are responsible for continuing to feel hurt if we keep thinking these ways.

When we learn to allow God's Word to replace our wrong thinking, to correct our outlooks and to renew our spirits with Spirit-led thinking we are then able to overcome these wrong mindsets. Ask the Lord to give you the wisdom to know how to change your thinking so you will not only be renewed, but also be transformed into actively looking at every situation with the mind of Christ Jesus[10]—not just now and then but all the time. If you honestly want transformation, the Holy Spirit will help you. Do you want to avoid stinking thinking? Then spend time regularly reading the Bible, and each time ask the Holy Spirit to speak to you. More than likely you will not have daily epiphanies, but your thinking will improve in direct proportion.

Here are some of the ways we lead ourselves astray. The first area many of us trip ourselves up is in thinking we have to be loved and accepted by those who are most important to us. Let me tell you, that mindset can be almost impossible to get past. When my wife told me she wanted a divorce, that she was not happy and was going to do whatever it took to find happiness, I was crushed. I knew that the depth of emotion behind her words was a deathblow. I was a failure as a husband. There was not anything I could do or say to make her love me and accept me. How was I going to go on without her? The truth is that there really was not anything I could do or say to change her mind. I had to let go of her, and instead focus on what God was trying to do in me. She did not leave, although she certainly could have done so.

Even if she had left and divorced me, I would still have been a man whom God loves. In other words, our worth as human beings is not predicated by how well other people accept or love us. It rests instead on the facts that we were made in God's image, and *he* loves us.

Going hand in hand with the notion that those most important to us have to love and accept us is the thought that we have to live up to others' expectations of us. If that is you, then ask yourself, "Is that how Jesus lived?" Most of the time he was shown neither love nor acceptance, yet he obeyed God and overcame the whole world.[11] That is not to say that we should walk around with a laissez-faire attitude, thinking, "So what if nobody likes me. I'll just keep doing my own thing." Jesus' motivation was not in pleasing himself. He was doing the will of his Father in heaven. If we are walking with the Lord, being obedient to the leading of his Spirit, then even if those we care most about do not accept us we will be able to rejoice anyway.

The trouble is that often we simply are not listening to his voice. We are preoccupied with our own thoughts. How did I get past my painful dilemma? I retreated to God, and chose to trust him over my own thoughts and those of my wife—regardless of the outcome. It was not easy, but I had to come to the point where I could trust him whether she stayed or left.

Thankfully the day came when I realized that I could accept myself as I am without being self-righteous. God accepts and loves me, so why shouldn't I? I do not have to try to live up to everybody else's expectations of me. I can simply be whom God made me to be—flaws and all—living for and seeking him, and be happy. It is very freeing!

But there have been times in my life when I felt I could not go on any more. It is difficult to describe the emotional impact of years of telling and trying to show my wife that I loved her, and in return never hearing her say back, "I love you." It was a very long and painful season when she could not utter those words, and it took a heavy emotional toll on me. You see, what I was longing for was her affirmation of love for me. My happiness depended on it, and because I did not get it I was not happy.

Thank God those days are gone, and yet I am oddly grateful for them because it was during those times that the love of Christ and the intimacy I now share with him carried me and helped me to keep on day by day. It was in that place that I learned with more than just my head that my joy comes from my relationship with God and not from my relationship with others. It frequently takes these hard places to bring us to get our eyes on God instead of on ourselves. King David, a man who understood hardship, spoke of this seeming contradiction when he said, "It is good for me that I have been afflicted, that I might learn Your statutes."[12]

A second area we sometimes fall short in—and one that I devoted a chapter to because it plagues so many of us—is in thinking that before we can feel happy about ourselves we must be perfectly competent and achieving whatever we think of as success. In other words, if I am not in control then I do not have a right to feel good about me. Wrong. God equips us, energizes us and enables us to be competent for everything *he* asks us to be, to do and to think. When God calls you he will equip you. Your responsibility is not to be perfect before you step out, but rather to trust God that he will enable you *as* you step out. Read what the apostle Paul had to say to his beloved brothers and sisters in Philippi:

"I know how to be abased and live humbly in straitened circumstances, and I know also how to enjoy plenty and live in abundance. I have learned in any and all circumstances the secret of facing every situation, whether well-fed or going hungry, having a sufficiency and enough to spare or going without and being in want. I have strength for all things in Christ Who empowers me [I am ready for anything and equal to anything through him Who infuses inner strength into me; I am self-sufficient in Christ's sufficiency]."[13]

Your worth, your ability, your fulfillment can never be met in your own strength or competence. Trying to do so will never satisfy for long if at all. It is only in Jesus that you will ever have your deepest longings satisfied. If you feel you must be a success before you can be happy, then you have again fallen into the trap of making yourself out to be a god and have just as equally set yourself up for unhappiness and a big fall.

Instead, derive your self-value and happiness not from within yourself but from God. King Solomon wrote "In all your ways know, recognize, and acknowledge Him, and He will direct and make straight and plain your paths. Be not wise in your own eyes ..."[14] More often than not that is easier said than done, because we still want to be in control. Instead, see your happiness and satisfaction in

God. If you will allow him to do so he will lead you in the right direction.

Yet another area in which we mislead ourselves is in thinking it is easier to avoid problems and responsibilities than to face them. I certainly understand this. It has been an area into which I have fallen all too often. Let's face it. It is uncomfortable to deal with our difficulties, and we just don't like being uncomfortable. Nevertheless, it is the coward's way out. It is not the right path.

There have been many times when I was behind in my bills that I would see on caller-id that the incoming phone call was from a bill collector, so I would not answer. There have been many times when I set the bills in a pile over in the corner of my desk and tried to simply ignore them. I unconsciously thought that if I did not pay attention to them then they would not bother me. That is not even a good try. I am sure you can think of at least one or two ways you have avoided responsibility or have tried to avoid facing a problem.

For the wrong reasons we mistakenly think if we just ignore our problems they will go away. They do not. More often they get worse when we do that. Because most of us are willing to pay a price for something we value, the question then becomes: if we really value being followers of Jesus Christ, then are we willing to deny ourselves of our assumed rights? Will we shoulder the cross of responsibilities that he assigns to us and follow him wherever he leads? Think hard before you answer. This is one of the main reasons many struggle so hard with committing their lives to Jesus. They do not want to have to do something they do not like or want to do, and know that if they are sold-out to God then they will have to willingly concede.

Another area of our stinking thinking concerns some of our thoughts of others—and this particular one we seem easily attracted to because it makes us feel better about ourselves. At one time or another we all have thought that certain people are just plain bad and therefore deserve punishment for their misdeeds—the father, brother, uncle, priest or friend who sexually abused you; the serial rapist or murderer, the street gang member who kills people for sport or to prove how macho he is, or the business executive who steals his employees' retirement funds. We can all come up with a list of those we think are just plain bad.

Unquestionably those behaviors are wrong and deserving of punishment, but while it may make you feel better about yourself to look at someone else's sins, you have no right to be their judge. Jesus—always our example—prayed for people who were not even seriously looking for God. He prayed for the adulteress, the tax collector and the thief. Instead of condemning them, he went to bat for those who needed to grow up spiritually, emotionally and mentally. He still does. Did Jesus condemn the woman brought to him who had been caught in the very act of adultery? As God he had every right to judge and condemn her, but instead he called into question the motives of those who were judging her. To the adulteress Jesus did not bring condemnation. He said simply, "I do not condemn you either. Go on your way and from now on sin no more."[15]

Our problem is that we look at others through our own frail, human eyes. In God's view, however, are any of us really better than anyone else? The answer, of course, is that we are not. The Bible tells us that God does not respect any one person over another based on his or her own inherent goodness.[16]

The way I see it there are only two classes: God the Creator of everything, and then everyone and everything else. We have no right to be self-righteous. Sin is sin— regardless of degree—yet we try to mask our own guilt by pointing at others. We say spiritually foolish things like, "Well, he's a murderer," or "That teacher had sex with one of her students. I would never do anything like that."

All we are really doing when we point at someone else's flaws is trying to deflect attention away from our own. We all too easily forget that as far as God is concerned missing the mark at all—whether it is something as trivial as having a bad thought or stealing a cookie, to something as major as molesting a child or murdering someone— disqualifies us. That is why we need a Savior and why we have no right to judge others. Without Jesus we all stand equally condemned.[17]

Granted, what we generally think of as evil behaviors is not acceptable, but neither is our improper and judgmental response. Perhaps we never would commit some heinous crime like sexual molestation; but we gossip, we judge and we get proud and self-righteous. Even Sister Theresa had her struggles. Instead of writing others off, we should follow Christ's example by praying for them. Sometimes that is easier said than done; nevertheless it is what we ought to do. Ask God to help you to pray for them. He is waiting, and he will help you.

Another type of all too common stinking thinking is worry. The worrier—not the warrior—thinks he or she must always be prepared for the worst and that the best way to be prepared is to constantly think about what might go wrong, what is wrong, what is dangerous or what should be feared. On the contrary, our thoughts should be filled with what is true, honorable, right, pure, lovely, excellent, admirable, just, gracious and worthy of praise. Instead of worrying, we should fix our thoughts on anything that is virtuous or worthy of praise.[18]

Instead of filling our minds with scenarios of the worst possible situations we ought to concentrate on letting love overcome our fears, our disappointments and our troubles.[19] We are admonished to be like caterpillars that metamorphose into butterflies. Our thought life needs to be transformed, renewed, our attitudes changed by right thinking and God's Word.[20]

You see, my friend, it comes back to what or whom we worship. Do we continue thinking consciously or subconsciously that we can change ourselves and therefore do not need God; or do we humble ourselves, worship the One who created us and trust him to change us as he sees fit? If our thoughts are centered on our problems, then we are focused on ourselves. If we think about the good in life, our hearts will naturally turn to God, and he will work the changes necessary in our hearts and in our lives.

Some, who may feel pangs of guilt for past behavior, think the past has molded us into who we are and that it is therefore too late to change. Often the drug addict or the alcoholic believes that even though he may want to change it is impossible for him to do so. Many of us think that same way about a variety of bad behaviors. God does not think so. God says that when we become a part of his family our previous moral and spiritual condition is gone. We are changed. We are made into new creatures.[21] Do you have a checkered past? Are there skeletons in your closet? If you have come to a saving knowledge of Jesus Christ then you are no longer the same. You are a new person.

You are not condemned to be a prisoner to your past. Instead, thank God, and let the past pass away. One of my favorite phrases in the Bible these days (used 396 times in the KJV of the Bible) is "and it came to pass," meaning that it (whatever your "it" is) did not come to hang around forever. It came, and it will leave. The apostle Paul wrote, "I do not consider, brethren, that I have captured and made it my own [yet]; but one thing I do [it is my one aspiration]: forgetting what lies behind and straining forward to what lies ahead, I press on toward the goal to win the [supreme and heavenly] prize to which God in Christ Jesus is calling us upward" (Philippians 3:13-14 AMP).

Things do not always go the way I planned, and when that happens, I feel terrible. Another of my weaknesses is exposed. Do you know what I mean? When the dog is out digging crater sized holes and turning my lawn into Swiss cheese—again; when the water valve in the toilet is broken, and the radiator in my car is leaking; when the pile of bills on the desk is still staring me in the face, and I've just come home to a house that has had the electricity shut off, when my daughter is in the hospital and my wife is telling me she wants a divorce, well, I have a tendency to think that everything about life is wrong and terrible.

This is one of the devil's favorite tactics—to get our minds off of what GOD can do, and focused instead on what is not going the way we think it should. Then again sometimes we just feel like whining. For example, one day I was complaining to my wife about what a rotten day I was having at work.

She responded with, "Honey, tomorrow is another day." There is nothing like a good cliché when I am feeling down.

I replied, "Yeah, but it isn't tomorrow yet!" She meant well, but it did not encourage me at all at the time. I did, however, need an attitude adjustment. My focus was on my problems, and I did not want to hear anything other than sympathy. Stinking thinking.

The truth is that God has the capacity to make all things work together for our good as long as we love him and fit into his plan.[22] The keyword there is together. You may be facing what appears to be the mother of all problems, but it is not the end of all things, you are not the first person or the only person to experience such a problem, and whatever it is, it is certainly not bigger than God.

When I reflect on my past, I now see that all the problems with which I have ever had to deal have been part of God's plan for me. Each and every issue—including the ones I am facing today, and still do not understand— were and are there for my betterment and to remind me of what an awesome God I serve. If we will awaken to our adversary's ruse, stop dwelling on the problem and instead focus our attention on the awesome power, character and promises of God, then our entire perspective will change. I am not saying that just thinking differently will solve our problems, but it certainly will help. It will help us through them by drawing us closer to God and helping us to mature more as his sons and daughters.

If we pass the test then we will not have to take it again. If we fail the test then sooner or later God will put us through it again and will keep doing so until we do pass it. God will not pass us along to the next grade just to push us on, as do some schools. He will make us repeat that troublesome grade until we pass the exam. Where God is concerned, it is in your best interests to become a quick learner.

Difficulties are a part of life. Some people seem to live calm, smooth lives, but I assure you everyone goes through difficult times. Sooner or later we all experience them. They are thrust upon some of us at very early ages, while for others the worst come late in life. Most of us have difficulties that range from minor to catastrophic off and on throughout our lives. I have known many people who seemed to be doing well, everything going right for them, when the truth was they were on the brink of divorce or in a place where their faith was about to go belly up. A calm exterior is not always a valid sign of an untroubled life. I encourage you to submit to God's chisel, allowing him to sculpt you.

Often we mistakenly believe we have no control over our happiness, that what determines whether or not we are happy is what happens to us. That is just plain wrong. Difficulties do not have to determine whether or not you are happy. While it is not often easy, I can now laugh even in the middle of major problems. Speaking to me one day about making arrangements to have our youngest sister's ashes flown to Hawaii, my older sister, said, "Maggie hasn't arrived yet." I laughed, and said, "Yes she has, even if her ashes haven't caught up. She's already in heaven." Little did I know that less than two years later this same oldest sister would die too. As she lay dying in the hospital we were all sad and cried, but we also joked, laughed, and relished in the comfort of each other.

We do not overcome because we have chosen to be happy. Those who overcome their difficulties have a way of doing so through what comes out of their mouths, the empowering of the Spirit and the Word of God.[23]

The prolific apostle Paul wrote:

"If you only look at us, you might well miss the brightness. We carry this precious Message around in the unadorned clay pots of our ordinary lives. That's to prevent anyone from confusing God's incomparable power with us. As it is, there's not much chance of that. You know for yourselves that

we're not much to look at. We've been surrounded and battered by troubles, but we're not demoralized; we're not sure what to do but we know that God knows what to do; we've been spiritually terrorized, but God hasn't left our side; we've been thrown down, but we haven't broken."
(2 Corinthians 4:7-9, The Message)

Using a wrestling analogy, you may find yourself thrown to the mat, but that does not mean you have been pinned for the count. Our adversary may have pressed up alongside us in the race, but he will not strip us of the prize. The victory has already been won. There is good reason that Paul wrote to the church in Ephesus, saying:

In conclusion, be strong in the Lord [be empowered through your union with Him]; draw your strength from him [that strength which his boundless might provides]. Put on God's whole armor [the armor of a heavy-armed soldier which God supplies], that you may be able successfully to stand up against [all] the strategies and deceits of the devil. For we are not wrestling with flesh and blood [contending only with physical opponents], but against the powers, against [the master spirits who are] the world rulers of this present darkness, against the spirit forces of wickedness in the heavenly (supernatural) sphere." (Ephesians 6:10-12 AMP)

Another area of our stinking thinking—especially for those of us in American culture in the 21st century—is that we so often think we have to find the quickest and most perfect solution to whatever problem we happen to be facing. Instead of once again trying to be in control, we must allow the Lord to work out his greater will in and through our lives according to his schedule rather than ours.

One of the clearest examples of this in the Bible was Joseph. He was hated by his brothers, almost murdered by them, sold into slavery, falsely accused and then thrown into prison where he sat for 13 years. Those who promised to help forgot him. He did not deserve any of what happened to him. Joseph could easily have given up hope and fallen into despair. Instead, he allowed God's greater will to be carried out through his life—and it took nearly twenty years before God's purposes were seen! In the end Joseph wound up the second most important man in Egypt and saved a growing Israel from starvation.[24]

Can you hang in there another day? With God's help and the right sort of thinking about whatever your predicament may be, I bet you can. When I am in the middle of a problem—or as is more often the case, problems—I have learned to run to God, to lean on his strength instead of my own, to listen for his whispers of love and assurance, and to say to myself, "This too shall pass."

Finally, some of us are just plain lazy in our thinking. Either that or we have been beaten down and have grown so weary that we simply give up. We think that it is easier just to keep doing things the way we have been doing them without taking on any new commitments. If that is you, then consider this. Do you know what happens to water when it stagnates? It turns bitter or sour. It becomes life draining instead of life sustaining. The same happens to us, and it is not God's will for us. He wants us to keep on growing, moving forward and giving out more love each day.

If you will take the Word of God into your heart by daily reading and meditating on it, then in turn it will produce in you a greater love for the Lord, for yourself and for those around you. Do not become afraid to risk loving more.

If you are caught up in a web of stinking thinking, what can you do? Well, if your car is running rough what do you do? You take it to the mechanic, and he gives it a tune up. The same goes for you. If your thinking is off, then you need a mental tune up. The apostle Paul told the Roman Christians to not go along with their old worldly ways of thinking, but to instead have their minds transformed, metamorphosed—like a caterpillar into a butterfly[25]—from our natural mind to the mind of Christ.

To transform your mind there are three things you need. First, when you are in the thick of problems and trials, instead of dwelling on what seems to be going wrong, remind yourself what God has already done. One of the things I love about King David's psalms is that he was honest with God. He poured out his problems, his lack of faith at times, his fears and his concerns as well as his joy. For the first nine verses of Psalm 77 David complains to God. At the end of verse nine he instructs the reader to pause and calmly think about that. Then he writes the meat of the psalm. Beginning in verse 11 he says, "I will [earnestly] recall the deeds of the Lord; yes, I will [earnestly] remember the wonders [You performed for our fathers] of old."

Why does David do this? I believe it was because he knew that reflecting on God's past actions would help him to learn the true character of God. Knowing God's character is paramount to trusting him. More importantly, however, remembering what God has done helps us to better determine whether or not his actions in our particular circumstance reveal him to be righteous or not. It is almost as if David was saying, "I will spend some time thinking about God's past actions in order to see if I can find something in them to calm me down."

Many of us try to follow logic in how we live, but life is not logical. For example, we may feel we exceeded performance in our jobs and therefore deserve a raise or a promotion, yet wind up out of work. Trying to force logic into every facet our lives is often the cause of much of our worry. This sort of thinking feeds upon itself. Self-sufficiency becomes cancerous.

One of my hardest and most oft repeated lessons is learning to take a deep breath, to give the situation some time and to come back to it when I can be less emotionally attached. Reflecting on what God has already done helps immensely in this regard.

The second thing you can do to help readjust or renew your thinking is to recognize that being anxious about the problem does not help. This is not to say that we should be careless about taking care of our families, our homes and so on. It does mean that we should have the kind of confidence in God that releases us from worry and anxiety. Jesus taught us that we should not worry about whether or not we will have sustenance and clothing.[26] I know at times this is a struggle, but the more you are chiseled the more you come to trust God.

He challenges us to recognize that life is more than these things. If God has given us life, will he not also take care of what we truly need? Jesus' instruction was not a suggestion. It was an imperative: stop being anxious! Allowing him to transform your mind will help you to avoid anxious thoughts.

Spending regular time reading the Bible and asking God what he has to say specifically to you is vital. If you only crack open your Bible to read a verse or two along with the pastor on Sunday morning, then your thinking will remain right where it is. Habitual diving into the Word is of utmost importance in keeping your mind in check.

Finally, cultivate spiritual relationships. It is vital for each of us to recognize that we cannot make it through life alone. We need each other. Seek out the community of care, those who reassure the broken, hurting and disenchanted. This should be the Church. Seek out those who have been seeking, listening to and obeying God for a good while. You will find them a tremendous help.

Ask the Lord to help you to bring every irrational assumption into obedience to the will of Christ. If you will do this, then the he will replace your irrational exuberance or discouragement with steadfastness and correct thinking.

I do not know who coined the line, but it is right on target: "Let the mind of the Master be the master of your mind." Paul wisely brought it all around to this:

> "So here's what I want you to do, accepting God's help. Take your everyday, ordinary life— your sleeping, eating, going-to-work, and walking-around life—and place it before God as an offering. Embracing what God does for you is the best thing you can do for Him. Don't become so well-adjusted to your culture that you fit into it without even thinking. Instead, fix your attention on God. You'll be changed from the inside out. Readily recognize what he wants from you, and quickly respond to it. Unlike the culture around you, always dragging you down to its level of immaturity, God brings the best out of you and develops well-formed maturity in you." (Romans 12:1-2, The Message)

The transformation of your thinking will not happen overnight. Like any other habit, wrong thinking takes time, consistency and effort to bring about habitual change. The word the apostle Paul used in Romans 12:2 ("be transformed") speaks of more than a mere addition. It "implies a radical, thorough, and universal change, both outward and inward ... entirely renewed."[27] If you will think on what God has already done, stop worrying about what is outside of your control and instead spend regular time in the Bible searching out what God has to say, if you will cultivate spiritual relationships with mature Christians and learn to depend on them to help you to grow, then slowly but surely your thinking will come around.

There is always hope, and God always wants the best for you—despite what you may think or feel. Learn to trust him. Listen for his whispers of love, and accept his hammer and chisel as he shapes you into the man or woman he has purposed you to be. I guarantee you will not regret it. Your life will be richer than you can imagine. The biggest battleground of all for us is in our own minds.

Chiseled by Trial

CALL ME HOSEA

To err is human. To forgive is not company policy.

Anonymous

Hosea was a prophet who lived about 2,700 years ago during the reigns of the last two kings of Israel. Often considered a prophet of doom, he spoke of the judgments that were to come upon Israel because of their unfaithfulness to God. More importantly, however, he also spoke of God's promise to restore them. At home, his life was a reflection of the spiritual life of Israel. Instead of devoting herself to her husband, his wife, Gomer, went after other men. As she was unfaithful to Hosea, the people of Israel were unfaithful to God, repeatedly chasing after other gods.

Relationships are so vital to God that in the first of his commandments he decreed that we are not to worship anyone or anything other than him.[1] Spiritual infidelity is one of the major themes of the Old Testament, and the full impact of Israel's unfaithfulness to God—which is true of humanity throughout history—became one of my major life learning experiences. Over the course of about five

137

years, the one who is "bone of my bone" chased after others. Do not dare to judge her. None of us is qualified to do so. Such behavior is never one-sided. Infidelity almost always has at least two causes—a husband *and* a wife. The only exception I can think of is between God and us because he never breaks his covenants.

When a relationship sours, it is usually because in some way both sides have failed. There isn't anything earth shattering about that—it unfortunately happens all too frequently. In my case, however, even though it was a time of indescribable pain, it became a time of drawing closer to God and of discovering a fuller understanding of mercy and grace.

This crucible forever changed my relationship with God because it was in that fire that I came to better see and understand his deeply intimate love. While my heart was ripped out it was there that he spoke to me. What he said was, "Now you know on a very small scale how much I hurt when even one person turns his or her back on me." The impact of those words forever changed me, and because of the resulting keener awareness of my own imperfections, I am now able to extend true forgiveness to others and to accept God's forgiveness for my many failures.

It was only after a long and serious time of soul-searching that I decided to write this chapter at all. I was concerned about what our children or other relatives and friends might think. My goal is not to tell a sordid tale, or to say or do anything that would demean my wife in any way. I deeply love her, so you will not find any details here because that is not what this chapter is about. I believe the Lord has assured me on several occasions that I should tell the story. He must have his good reasons.

Jesus Christ charges me to love her the same way he loves the Church. That is, to the point of setting all of my wants or desires aside. I am not to love her any less than that, and after all, I am no better than is she. While many of us are unwilling to admit we are any worse than someone else—or even on equal standing—the truth of the matter is that we are all sinners, and it is only by the grace of God that any of us has the ability to even breathe.

Many men and women whose spouses are unfaithful to them turn to anger and bitterness, to drugs or the bottle, or to an affair of their own. From our perspective that may be understandable: their trust was broken, they were betrayed and even violated. They are deeply wounded. I understand those feelings. The hurt, however, goes deeper than most can imagine. It is our human nature to become defensive, and in many cases aggressive, when hurt or threatened with physical or emotional injury. That is not God's way, and we can see this quite clearly in his dealings with Israel over the centuries.

Time after time his chosen people behaved like prostitutes by chasing after other gods, yet God was patient with them. The Bible says that he is waiting to forgive, that he does not easily become angry and he possesses great and steadfast love.[2] This is vastly different from the way we think we should treat those who hurt us.

In each case God's patience eventually came to an end, and he levied judgment. The people then realized the wickedness of what they had done and turned back to God who then restored their relationship with him. We just do not think that way, and so I asked, "Why? Why did you forgive them? Why continue to accept a person who is habitually unfaithful?" I mean, really, why didn't God just kill them off?

To bring it back to a personal level, conventional wisdom tells us that if your spouse has an affair it is wiser to divorce him or her and go on with your life without having to deal with the pain of unfaithfulness. It is not worth the effort to try to rebuild trust—if you ever can—after your spouse has an affair. Right? After all, that kind of emotional pain is one of the hardest to endure. It insidiously and constantly gnaws at your heart, taking its toll on you both emotionally and physically. Many of us today consider it wiser to simply end such a relationship and be done with it. Write the other person off and go on with life hopefully having learned something.

But that is not God's way. It is the easy way, but also the wrong way. If my wife was unfaithful to me, who am I to judge her? I had been unfaithful to her many years earlier. I certainly had—and still have—many of my own faults and failures that just as easily condemn me. Remember the childhood wisdom about pointing your finger at someone else? When we do so, we have more fingers pointing back at us.

Who are we, after all, to decide whether someone is worthy of our forgiveness? I mean, do we charge for forgiveness? We must forgive, but also understand that when we do forgive, we accept within us the consequences of the wrongs of others. Think about that for a moment. It means you accept the pain, the burden and the problems that come with the wrong that was done to you. Frankly, forgiveness is not easy, but it is what God commands of us.

A sobering thought is that, because he loves us, God took on himself the pain, burden and problems of our spiritual unfaithfulness. He willingly and freely forgave me; therefore I am obliged to do the same for others. The apostle Peter reminds us that even when we were sinking in the ugliness of our own sin, Jesus came and redeemed us. He bought us back as Hosea did with Gomer; only Jesus did so not with money but with the most precious of all things, his own sinless blood.[3]

What did God give for you? It was not any sort of worldly wealth. He gave his son. Jesus took upon himself the full burden of our wrongdoings, our sin. Why then do we think we have any right to hang onto the wrongs others have done to us? What makes us think we are good enough to decide that the cost to us is too high to pay, or worse, that the one who hurt us is not worth forgiving? Take it a step further. God commands us to forgive those who do us wrong, and he says that if we do not forgive them then he will not forgive us.[4]

A beautiful passage in the book of Isaiah (one of Hosea's contemporaries) speaks of pardon and forgiveness. In it, God says to us that his thoughts and ways are not the same as ours.[5] Many of us have heard that passage many times, but we too often take it out of its context:

forgiveness. It is not so much a comparison of our level of intelligence with his but of God's forgiveness compared to ours. When it comes to forgiveness, the plans and purposes of God are so far above our ways and our thinking. When we refuse to forgive, we are in effect saying that we are at least equal with God, if not superior. This is yet another of our vain attempts to make ourselves the ultimate authority over our lives. God will not stand for that.

We find it hard to forgive. Often we either desire or actively seek revenge, or we feign forgiveness and try just to sweep it all under the rug. Many hold on to bitterness. Most of us, at least for a time, get self-righteous. We may say we forgive while secretly hoping that at the very least God will repay them for whatever it was they did to us. In other words, we say we forgive, but we want God to do the dirty work for us and make sure they "get what's coming to them." Again, that is not God's way. He has no desire for revenge. He does not harbor any malice. He has no reluctance to forgive. Truly, it is amazing grace. It is like watching clouds. They form shapes, move, and change in moments. In no time at all, we cannot remember the shapes of any of them. That is how I perceive God's remembrance of our sins. Once we seek his forgiveness, he forgives and never remembers them again. That isn't to say he is forgetful, but that he chooses to forget when we repent.

If we read the Bible, one important lesson many of us miss is the connection between Israel's unfaithfulness to God, and Jesus' response to the disciple Peter when he asked how many times he should forgive. Thinking self-righteously, he dared to suggest to Jesus that perhaps he should forgive seven times. I can imagine him thinking, "Isn't it big of me to not only offer to forgive once, but even up to *seven* times?" That was a huge 700 percent increase! Jesus' response, I think, put him in his proper place. He told him to forgive seventy times seven![6]

Most of us miss his message there because we are focused on doing the math. What Jesus was saying was to keep on forgiving. It is not a matter of seven times, forty-nine times, or a million times. Don't put a number on how often to forgive. Take that idea, and go back and revisit the relationship between God and the ancient Israelites. God kept on forgiving. Yes, he brought judgment (he does, after all, have the right and we do not), but every time they repented, he forgave and restored them. He is such a loving God. He longs to forgive us.

Going back to seventy times seven, we often think that the number of offenses has some sort of significance. We might forgive once, but if the offense reoccurs, we are slower to forgive, if we do at all. That is our nature. If someone offends us a third or even a fourth time, we refuse altogether to forgive. Thankfully, God is not like us. No matter how many times we have violated him, he is both able and willing to extend forgiveness to us. More importantly, it is precisely his desire to do so.

If what another does to us is slight, we are more likely to forgive than if we perceive the offense to be great. It is easier for us to forgive someone who slaps us than it is to forgive if they shoot us. We find it easier to forgive the person who fails to repay us the $20 borrowed than to forgive the executives who run off with our retirement funds. Again, this is not the case with God. He will extend forgiveness to us regardless of the severity of our offenses. Do not, however, think that means we can live lives of habitual sin, and just go running to beg forgiveness. We must repent—turn 180 degrees around from our unholy behaviors—and then we find that God is not only longing to forgive us, he is also just to forgive us.

When my heart was wrenched from me, when I thought the pain was more than I could endure, he spoke not words of comfort, but from Scripture words of command saying, "Love her even as Christ loves the Church." Let me tell you, that does not come naturally. It is not a mere suggestion to experience warm fuzzy feelings about your wife. It is a command to husbands. It is a command to sacrifice yourself *for her*. We husbands are to put our desires and needs behind us, and instead give ourselves to our wives. That is rarely a simple task.

In my case, it meant I had to let go of even my pain and suffering. I had to push it aside. Initially my flesh—my natural man—wanted to cast her aside, to seek revenge on both her and her lovers. Repeatedly hearing God's voice and commands kept me from that course. Instead, with his help, I set my hurt and anguish aside and loved her even when she did not love me. Let me tell you, that really does require the intervention of God in one's life. I was not a saint about it either. Sometimes I drank to dull the pain, but that only made things worse. One afternoon I wound up throwing a folding chair across the yard and screaming at the top of my lungs. God was with me even there, and he was forgiving me while I was struggling to forgive her.

So how do you forgive someone who has betrayed you? First, you make the choice to do so. As I said, it does not come naturally. You have to actively choose to forgive. We selfishly want to think we are so much better than the other person. We want to make them pay for what they did to us. We even want to wallow in our anguish. Those are not the behaviors God desires of us. I could never have forgiven my wife if not for three things: I chose to forgive her, I sought God's help, and I reminded myself often that I am really not any better of a person.

Choosing to forgive is vital, but it is not sufficient by itself. We must come to the place of trust in God where we can release the individual who has hurt us into his care. I can no more make someone willingly behave the way I want them to than I can to make myself grow another inch in height. I can only change myself—and even then only with God's help.

Forgiveness was something I had to choose to do, and with that I had to seek God's help. That meant I had to stop trying or even wanting to change her. It meant not expecting her to come to me asking my forgiveness. It meant seeing the good that is in her—and there is so much good there—focusing instead on that and desiring God's will in her life rather than my will. It meant coming to the place where even if she left me or continued to have affairs, that I would trust God was working in her life. What did Hosea do when Gomer left him and went chasing other men? He went and redeemed her. He literally bought her back off the slave blocks just as Christ did for us and as he commands husbands to do for their wives.

If you have been divorced do not despair, and do not get angry with me for saying that it is not God's desire. He does hate divorce, but he does not hate those who get divorced. He hates divorce because he knows how much it hurts so many people. It is because relationships are vital to him (and to us, whether or not we realize it) that he hates divorce. He is a loving father who takes no joy in seeing his children hurt.

Occasionally divorce is warranted. I will probably take some heat from some people for saying that, but I believe it is true. For example, where there is a chronically abusive spouse, and after serious help has been sought and ignored, divorce may be the only realistic option. Such cases, however, should be rare exceptions. I dare say that when over 40% of marriages end in divorce something is terribly wrong with how we perceive the importance of relationships. Those who are divorced can be encouraged that he is willing to forgive if we will acknowledge our failure and return to him.

Most of us already know that when we harbor ill will toward another person that bitterness falls on us instead. It also affects those around us. We can quite literally ruin our health and peace because we are bitter, angry and unforgiving. On the other hand, the person who we are angry with may be completely unaware of our feelings and go on with his or her life totally unaffected, while we continue to live a life without peace and even of degrading health.

God was merciful to me, because I was merciful to my wife. Country-Western singer Garth Brooks had a song that says, "We buried the hatchet, but left the handle sticking out." If you want to trip yourself up, that is one sure way to accomplish the goal. We should not keep going back to grab the axe handle. When we forgive, we are to forgive completely, and that means burying the hatchet *and* the handle. More often than not that requires consciously and repeatedly forgiving until we can extend full and unconditional forgiveness.

Decades ago after my adultery, my wife would often lay her hands on me as I slept, choosing to instead forgive and pray for me. The choice to forgive in turn releases us from judgment and can be the impetus to bring a restored and even a renewed relationship.

Love her. As The Message puts it, "Husbands, go all out in your love for you wives, exactly as Christ did for the church—a love marked by giving, not getting" (Ephesians 5:25). So just how did Christ love his bride, the Church? By now we ought to know he gave himself for her, but what does that mean beyond the obvious. He laid down his life. This goes beyond just setting your own wants, needs and desires aside and preferring your wife. Jesus came and gave himself in order to save the Church. It is our duty and moral obligation as husbands to not only protect and provide for our wives. It is equally our duty to promote their salvation and to build them up.

Husbands want and need respect from their wives, but that respect is not an inalienable right. Men who put the spiritual and physical wellbeing of their wives above their own desires earn it. Jesus actively worked to save us. He did not just tell us he loved us. He did not just have the warm-fuzzies about us. He demonstrated his love for us. Therefore, we husbands also have to work at loving our wives.

Philosophy or theology can be intellectually entertaining, but let us be practical. How do we love our wives sacrificially? What do we do? When you come home from work and you just want to plant yourself on the couch for a while and watch the news, and you see the dishwasher hasn't been emptied, put your desire to relax aside for a few minutes and put the clean dishes away. If the sink is full of dirty dishes, rinse them off and put them in the dishwasher after you empty it. That is a simple act any of us can do, and it only takes a few minutes. Oh, and do not go bragging to your wife about having done that. Do not do it so she will notice and thank you. Just do it. Anything you see that needs doing around the house, do it for her. Just be sure to get your responsibilities squared away as well.

If you are out in public, and your wife says something about you that you think is derogatory, bite your tongue. Instead of correcting her (she may not have meant what you thought), think of something you can say that will instead build her up. Strengthen her; make her feel better about herself and her relationship with you. When you get home from a long day at work, do not start a conversation by complaining about what a hard day you had or asking what is for dinner. Compliment her instead on her beauty, her ability as a mother and a wife, how good it is to come home to her where you can be her knight of the castle.

That may sound a little sappy, but the point here is to be realistic by actively seeking ways to encourage and build up your wife even when she does not respond as you would like. The more you do it the more naturally it will come to you, and the more she will feel secure in your love of her.

On a more difficult level, loving your wife sacrificially takes a lot more effort and learning to hear what God is saying in the moment. What do you do if you discover she is having an affair? Do you start a big argument? No. You will have to confront her, but fighting will not fix anything. It will only make it worse. Do you quietly file for a divorce? It is not popular in today's culture to say no, but that is what God says. Jesus told the religious leaders of that day that the only reason God allowed for divorce under the Mosaic Law was because the men were so obstinate about it.[7]

As I said a little while ago, relationship is paramount to God, and so it should be with us. That does not mean that working through the problem of infidelity and rebuilding trust and a strong relationship is anything simple. Quite the contrary; it is very difficult because we have to die to our selfish desires. We want to vent our anger. We want revenge. We want to hurt the other person. We want to make them pay or suffer for what they did to us. We want them out of our life. We want. We want. We want. That is not God's way. If we are to be godly leaders in our homes—both as husbands and as fathers—then we must become imitators of God.

In my case, God had to work on me for several years. Repeatedly his word came to me, "Love her as Christ loved the Church..." That is a hard order to submit to when the person you love does not seem to love you anymore. I had to abandon my own selfish desires and learn to love my wife by treating her with respect and honor, preferring her above others (even when the temptation was not to), and to sincerely pray for her.

The breakthrough for me came when I finally let go. For several years I thought I was being a good husband simply by forgiving her and giving her what she did not deserve. When the light finally dawned on me, I discovered that what I really needed to do was to let go. I had been trying to bring about change in her through my own efforts, and that just doesn't work. I let go of her, releasing her completely into God's hands. That meant that even if she ultimately left me, I had to willing still trust that God held her in his hands. Once I finally let go, stopped trying to change her and allowed God to take over, change came ... in his time. It also took seeking him to change me. Change in her might not have ever come, and I had to willing to accept that outcome too.

Loving our wives as Christ loves the Church requires an active, conscientious effort. It means daily, and sometimes even minute-by-minute, choosing to show our love in realistic ways; which, by the way, includes not demanding that she behave the way we think she ought to. Just as do we men, she answers to God for her behavior, not to us.

While our emotions are God-given blessings, love is not so much how we feel about another. It is more importantly our actions. Do I seek a divorce, or do I give up myself and try to win her back? It is not about who is right and who is wrong. That just comes back to self. "You hurt me, so I cannot love you anymore." There is nothing at all noble about that.

Like it or not the truth is that kind of thinking is selfish. Instead, we are commanded (it is not a suggestion) to show our wives the kind of love Jesus exhibited for us. He set himself aside, and suffered and died for us—a people who are completely undeserving. Are you getting fidgety yet? You should.

Extremely rare is the man who selflessly loves his wife. Most of us are self-centered. Jesus knew what he was doing, and he knew what it would cost him in anguish, pain, and suffering; and yet he willingly pressed on and took it all because he loves us. He loved us sacrificially. He loved us in very painfully real and active ways. He endured shame. He suffered. He died. He did it all because having a relationship with you and me was that important to him.

He could have justifiably tossed us aside as so many do with their wives or husbands. After all, he was not guilty of anything. We were, but he took the burden of our wrongs upon himself so that we would clearly see his love for us and so that he could restore a right relationship with us. That is what "Love her as Christ loved the Church" is all about—rebuilding, bringing healing and restoring that broken relationship because of real love, sacrificial love, knowing the cost. Yes, there is truth and judgment, but there is also grace and mercy. If we lean too far in either direction, we fall. We must, with God's help, properly balance truth and mercy.

THEY KILL THEIR OWN

Many that live deserve death.
And some that die deserve life.
Can you give it to them? Then do not be too eager to deal out
death in judgment. For even the very wise cannot see all
ends.

J.R.R. Tolkein

Before I begin, be warned that this chapter may be divisive. It *is* disturbing. My intention is not to stir up division or strife, but rather to awaken us to the fact that as both the Church and as individuals some serious self-examination is in order. Where is our accountability?

Something peculiar occurs in Africa with frequency. A spotted hyena gives birth to more than one cub. That is not what is odd. What most of us would not expect is that within minutes the two siblings, with fully developed incisors and canines will be doing everything within their power to kill one another. It happens not only in the wild but even when they are born in captivity. Most of us might wonder about that for a moment, and then move on to other thoughts.

What puzzles me, however, is that like the hyenas, some churches—the very places that should be havens of forgiveness, healing and hope—become little clubs where those in real need are considered outsiders, a threat to survival, and consequently are crushed rather than accepted, helped and restored. I cannot even begin to describe the hurts that so many have expressed to me that they received at the hands of people who claim to be followers of Christ. I too have born more than my share of pain at the hands of fellow Christians.

If you happen to think that this sorry behavior is something new, think again. During the Passover celebration the very night before the crucifixion, Jesus' disciples argued among themselves about who would be the greatest.[1] The Amplified version of the Bible refers to it as "an eager contention." Can you imagine that? There was Jesus, telling them that he was about to leave them, about to suffer and die, but instead of being concerned about his immanent departure they were fighting about which of them was the most important! Skip ahead a few decades, and we find the apostle Paul needing to admonish Christians in Corinth about their envy, strife and divisions.[2] James and the writer of Hebrews also wrote about strife, and Paul went so far in his letter to Christians in Galatia to include it in his list of "works of the flesh," saying,

> "Now the doings (practices) of the flesh are clear (obvious): they are immorality, impurity, indecency, Idolatry, sorcery, enmity, strife, jealousy, anger (ill temper), selfishness, divisions (dissensions), party spirit (factions, sects with peculiar opinions,

heresies), Envy, drunkenness, carousing, and the like. I warn you beforehand, just as I did previously, that those who do such things shall not inherit the kingdom of God" (Galatians 5:19-21 NASB).

That was written almost 2,000 years ago to a group of Christians—people who believed in Jesus and who had already learned basic doctrines. It doesn't sound like it though. Not a lot has changed over the centuries. I am sorry to say I have seen all of Paul's "doings of the flesh" in varying degrees in a number of churches—and almost unbelievably all of it in one particular congregation. Paul's words are as applicable today as they were then, because all too often our self-centered natures still dominate our behavior. I am not alone in this thinking. Christian author, Philip Yancey said in his book "What's So Amazing About Grace?"[3]

> Oddly, I sometimes find a shortage of grace within the church, an institution founded to proclaim, in Paul's phrase, "the gospel of God's grace."

It is a sad fact that some Christians hurt people. Some people bring hurt upon themselves by their unrealistic expectations or their own behavior, but that does not diminish the hurt we do to each other. The truth is that each of us who professes Jesus Christ as our Lord will answer to God for our actions, our reactions, our judgments and our mistreatment of others—regardless of whether or not such treatment seemed justifiable to us at the time.

In contrast to many in churches today, Jesus preferred the company of the kinds of people most of us do not like; those who do not pretend to be super spiritual and who are obviously full of big problems: those who are sexually active outside of marriage, get drunk, tell lies, steal or cheat, the unkempt and unfashionable, the broken and the flawed.

Many of us today turn our noses up at similar groups: people with tattoos, smokers, those who drink alcohol, those who come to church in jeans or shorts, men with long hair or women with extremely short hair, ex-convicts, the person everyone "knows" is sexually promiscuous, or the one who lets slip every once in a while—or even often— with "colorful language."

All too many of us shun street people, the homeless, the poor, the dirty—those who are in real need. Many of us feel justified in thinking judgmentally about these people. After all, we say to ourselves, they are sinners. They are not spiritual like us. They deserve what they have received.

In the eyes of God, none of us is any better than anyone else. Like it or not, God loves them whether or not we do. Jesus came and died for them just as he did for us. Those who think they are above that may say they love the unlovely—perhaps they will even greet them at the door of a church with a smile and a welcome—but you can bet most of them do not want "those" people in their backyard. Rest assured that some day we will answer for our treatment of those who needed Christian charity more than a condemning look, word or attitude.

A mindset here in the south seems to go along the lines that you can say whatever you wish about someone else just as long as you preface it with, "Bless his (or her) heart." "Bless her heart. Everyone just knows she's sleeping around." "Bless his heart; he just drinks all the time." When did we start believing that constitutes Christian behavior? Some people may believe it is okay to think and behave that way, but it is not.

The Pharisees, the religious leaders during Jesus' earthly life, accosted his disciples and asked them why he ate with those who were so obviously unrighteous—the tax collectors and sinners. Jesus heard their question and replied that the ones who need a doctor are those who are sick, not those who are well.[4] The world today is just as full of those kinds of people as in Jesus' days—probably even more so. Obviously, his point aimed at the religious elite, was that the very people they disapproved of were the ones for whom he came: those who were willing to recognize their failures and their need, unlike some of the self-righteous still with us today.

These religious leaders did not think they needed healing. They felt they had already arrived, that they were well and whole. They believed they were categorically better and that they must avoid these others who were sick. Unfortunately, many in the Church today still have this same mindset. Had I not been an eyewitness to the following events, I would never believe they could have happened. I assure you they are each true. Like hyena pups, all too often we Christians wound and kill our own and drive the lost away.

We, as the Church, are supposed to be a haven for those who are broken and hurt, those who are wandering through life. God commands Christians everywhere to serve the needs of the world, not to be a "bless me" club for an exclusive few who meet some manmade religious view of what makes a person worthy of God. The bottom line is that there isn't anything in any of us that can ever make us worthy of God's love and forgiveness. It is only by the blood of Jesus Christ that we can come before God as his sons and daughters, forgiven and restored to a right standing with him.

In 1997, after my family relocated from New Hampshire to Tennessee, we spent a couple of months looking for a church to call home. Some in Nashville have referred to this area as the belt buckle of the Bible belt. I was soon to see it an entirely different way. We visited several churches in the area, but the one that seemed to be the right place had a moderate congregation of about a hundred or so. At one time it had been what is now termed a mega-church with a membership that numbered in the thousands, and it was a focal point in the southeast for the Charismatic movement. Due to several nasty splits, by the time we arrived the congregation had dwindled.

The pastor, a recent transplant from up north, was a fiery and animated preacher. Throughout his sermons he paced back and forth across the stage, arms in constant motion. He was well educated and appeared to be serious about being a minister. He was also the negative stereotypical Charismatic minister. You know the kind— one who could almost convince his followers that he had seen green angels on red bicycles. Of course, he never made such a claim, but I think you get the idea.

At first, we enjoyed his preaching. His sermons included an abundance of Bible verses to support whatever point he was making at the time, and a lot of his preaching at first sounded right on target. Do not let a minister who can quote the Bible fool you. While a pastor ought to know Scripture well enough to quote it, being able to do so does not automatically make him or her right. Even the devil knows Scripture and can quote it better than any of us can. (Hence Paul's praise of those in Berea who "searched the scriptures daily" to determine if what they were being taught was correct.[5]) Little did we know just how fiery this pastor would prove himself to be once his true colors were revealed.

We began the process of fitting in and building relationships. Several of the members became close to us, and made us feel comfortably at home. It was a good start, but before three years had passed we were involved up to our eyeballs with a power-crazed pastor and his wife. When it was all over my wife was severely wounded emotionally, beat up by the modern day pharisaic elders who were filled with pride, prejudice, and ignorance, and I was in a state of complete shock. The flock was scattered, and the church vaporized in total collapse.

Back to the beginning. The mist slowly began to lift, and I began to see signs of serious problems. Without getting specific, the pastor was more concerned about his wife's preeminence than in tending to his flock, the congregation. Even without being privy to what went on behind the closed-door meetings of the elders, it was evident to most that there was very little agreement—if any—between the pastor and the elders. It did not take long for the pastor's disdain of them to appear in his sermons. He did not dance around his dislike, or even make veiled insinuations. In very unfriendly and clear terms he loudly stated where there were disagreements. That is not the behavior of a shepherd of God's flock.

While I do not expect total agreement between elders and a pastor on all matters all of the time, there should be general agreement based on common values and doctrinal beliefs, and when differences of opinion do come up they should prayerfully come to a peaceful compromise. There was little agreement between this pastor and the elders. That he would publicly call them derogatory names in his sermons was to me clear evidence of a man controlled by his personal ambitions rather than by his desire to serve God. By definition, a minister is supposed to be a servant,[6] not a king. This man, on the other hand, appeared to want nothing less than a kingdom, and his actions showed that he had no qualms at all about trampling over anyone who got in his way.

One Sunday morning my jaw fell into my lap while seated on one of the back rows next to one of these elders. As the pastor was once again verbally attacking them from the pulpit, the elder sitting next to me opened his mouth and intentionally said loudly enough for me to hear, some very filthy words about the pastor: "That &^@#*'s got to go!" This man later on became the church's business administrator, sexually harassed my wife and extorted large sum of money before finally being arrested. Yes, it shocked me too.

There were public confrontations on more than one occasion between the pastor and the elders during worship services. The pastor was out of control, and unfortunately so were the elders. While the pastor's bad behavior was out in the open for all to see, the elders were equally out of control, but their failures were not quite so obvious and were due to inaction and silence. How very sad, and yet what a clear picture of a colossal failure to be led by the Holy Spirit.

Eventually this minister took matters into his own hands. As is normal for the articles of incorporation used by almost every church in America, the by-laws of this church body had very clearly delineated how and who governed the church. For those unaware of the importance of such a document, it forms a civil and legally binding contract. It is not just church politics. Eventually the state of Tennessee had to step in and uphold it.

This document stated what powers the board of elders had, what powers the pastor had, and the exact processes to follow in the governance of the church. The pastor, however, didn't care about the articles of incorporation. If I remember correctly, he once stated they were meaningless. He seemed determined to run the entire show, and with an iron hand. For him it was not about serving. It was about power, control, and money.

A pastor (a shepherd of God's people) is supposed to take care of the congregation, the flock. He is to teach and feed them from God's Word. He is to protect and look out for them. He is to go after them when they wander, and bring them back.[7]

This minister, on the other hand, was a gossip. He shared with other pastors across town the dirty details of the lives of those who came to him for counsel. If he could get what he perceived as acclaim from his peers in other churches, he would make a point of blurting it out. Disgracefully some of those pastors enjoyed hearing his stories, which in turn only served to encourage him to continue such breaches of trust. I am ashamed to say there were only a few who would not entertain his gossip and in some cases outright lies about others. Other than perhaps movie screenwriters, who would have ever thought a minister would—like a teenage boy to his friends after a hot date the night before—share the confidential discussions of those who came to him for counseling?

Perhaps it should not have come as a surprise. Jesus warned us to, "Be wary of false preachers who smile a lot, dripping with practiced sincerity. Chances are they are out to rip you off some way or other. Don't be impressed with charisma; look for character." (Matthew 7:15, The Message). Other versions of the Bible refer to them as "savage wolves," which I think is quite an appropriate analogy.

Shortly before his death, the apostle Paul warned the church overseers in Ephesus of the same thing. He said, "I know that after I am gone, ferocious wolves will get in among you, not sparing the flock; Even from among your own selves men will come to the front who, by saying perverse (distorted and corrupt) things, will endeavor to

draw away the disciples after them [to their own party]"
(Acts 20:29-30 AMP).

This man and his wife were most assuredly a pair of
savage wolves. Their whole plan was to rip into this flock
and draw the people after them. Before the dust settled
most of the congregation had been scattered, some
maimed, some spiritually killed, with this man and his wife
not a caring for even one of them unless there was a profit
to make.

It got worse. I realize this sounds like a bad movie, but
it was all too real. Picture a guest speaker at a worship
service brazenly sowing seeds of discord by drawing a
bloodline across the sanctuary with a long double-edged
sword, calling people to take sides.

Imagine a woman during the sermon taking off her
shoes and violently throwing them at an interim minister,
narrowly missing the head of an elderly woman. I tell you
it happened.

Had I not been a witness it never would have entered
my mind for the wife of an elder during communion
service to go out to the parking lot and key the cars of
every one of the church's leaders. (Taking a key and
dragging it across the body panels of a car in order to
deeply scratch, scar and deface the vehicle is called
"keying.") My car bore its scars for several years.

Have you ever seen a pastor physically shove a person
aside who was praying for another? As justification for
such a rude and unwarranted act, he later stated that he
"can't have just anyone" praying for others in church, and

that as the pastor he was the only one who knew what was best. Excuse me? Did Jesus ever say that only an ordained minister might pray for another person?

On the contrary we are instructed that we "... ought always to pray and not to turn coward (faint, lose heart, and give up)."[8] The apostle Paul admonished us to "Pray at all times (on every occasion, in every season) in the Spirit, with all [manner of] prayer and entreaty. To that end keep alert and watch with strong purpose and perseverance, interceding in behalf of all the saints (God's consecrated people)" (Ephesians 6:18 AMP). It seems clear to me what we are supposed to do—pray for one another.

Would you expect to see a woman supposedly in the guise of helping another, jump off the stage, mat-slam a man who had asked for prayer, knock him to the floor in a spread-eagle move, straddle him with her legs, and begin screaming and pounding on him with her fists? My mouth fell open when I saw that happen. It was just so unbelievable I could barely trust my own eyes. To me, it is a powerful image of how some supposedly Christian people judgmentally, critically, emotionally and even sometimes physically treat many who are lost, hurting, or in the thick of some sort of crisis.

An affair between a woman and an associate minister was exposed. She admitted her guilt and sincerely sought the forgiveness of her husband, the elders and the pastor. Her husband forgave her, but the elders coldly rejected her. Rather than forgiving and offering godly counsel, they gossiped about her. The pastor outright refused to forgive, and in his self-righteous bitterness spread vicious lies about her. It is no surprise that she left that place broken emotionally, mentally and spiritually. The miracle is that she ever entered the doorway of a church again.

Today she remains close to God, restored to both him and her husband. Her husband and her former lover are today brothers in Christ who have a strong bond of affection for each other—one that will likely never be broken. Both men will publicly tell you they deeply love each other. How can that be? It is simply because those directly involved humbled themselves. Rather than insisting on having their own ways they sought God and his forgiveness. He, in turn, intervened and turned what was a tragedy into a triumph. God was victorious, and he gets the acclaim for bringing good out of a bad situation. How could I possibly know such private information? The woman was my wife.

One of the elders—the very one who intentionally used vulgar language in reference to the then senior minister—was a convict on parole who wound up stealing a large sum of money from the church. At the time of his appointment, none of the church leaders knew that because none of them had bothered to check his background before giving him the keys to the church bank accounts.

None of the elders would listen to warnings and complaints about this man's sexual harassment of the church's receptionist. He was an elder, and therefore above reproach—or so it was if you were one of the other elders who could not be bothered actively to oversee the governance of the church in anything other than name.

The administrator's theft was the deathblow for that church assembly. With the banks coming after them, and in order to save their own necks because they were personally liable, the board of elders literally gave the church facilities and grounds to another organization. What had at one time been a large bastion of spiritual growth; a focus of outreach not only to the surrounding community but to the entire world, had turned inward, rotted out and died.

Thinking back over those events, I would never have imagined such outlandish, childish and un-Christian behavior; and yet amazingly I witnessed each of those episodes. Granted, they were extremes of behavior. Most churches in America have neither such intense nor so many problems. There are many good men and women, both as members of congregations and in leadership in churches, who love others and seek to serve them. I am very pleased to say that the church my wife and I attend today has good men and women who visibly seek to serve God and others, whose desire is to heal the wounded and mend the broken, to help those who are disenchanted, disheartened or who have been hurt by other Christians. It is often, as the Church should be, a haven of hope and love.

Up to this point, we have seen a power-crazed minister, a group of elders who were running on autopilot and had become unable to hear God any longer, and a greedy and dishonest administrator. The next man we will look at was one type the public far too often hears about on the news— one who cannot control his response to sexual attractions.

Keep in mind that these men were coming into and going out of my life like a series of scenes in a bad dream, one right after another. The motivation here is not to point a finger at individuals, but to show that there are some serious problems going on in more than just one church. I know that any of us is just as capable of failing to live as we should.

I am no longer angry with any of these people— although I was for a season. I have forgiven each of them, and several I would gladly greet with a hug and a genuine smile at seeing them again.

Billy was the pastor of a well-known church, but at one point was accused of improper conduct with women. The leaders of the church asked him to leave. He did so reluctantly, and a short time later started another church. A few years passed, and then three women accused him of improper sexual conduct. Did he learn and correct his behavior? Did he seek help with his weakness? No, he instead offered weak excuses and empty explanations.

Nevertheless, people wanted to believe him, so they looked the other way and did their best to trick themselves into believing he was a victim. We as a congregation failed also because, instead of properly counseling him in order to help and restore him, we swept it all under the rug. We threw accountability to the wind just to get the dirty laundry out of public view.

I will admit that I was not in his congregation at the time, and therefore am not qualified to comment with any authority on what actually happened with the first accusation. I am merely stating what he has already publicly said to me. The background is now set.

Then Billy had at least one affair that I know about. There were secret meetings, sordid emails and a petting session in a car in a church parking lot. Several months later, and in tears, he apologized to the woman's husband. Unfortunately, they were crocodile tears. He concluded his whispered apology with "but we never went to bed." In other words, he ended his confession by trying to minimize what he had done.

He was not taking full responsibility for his decisions and behavior. It struck me as hauntingly similar to former President Bill Clinton's attempts to wriggle out of his adultery by trying to explain that he had not lied depending on how one defines the word "is." What makes some men think it is okay for them to behave this way? I do not understand.

Such impotent logic does not carry any weight with God. The Bible still quotes Jesus saying, "But don't think you've preserved your virtue simply by staying out of bed. Your heart can be corrupted by lust even quicker than your body. Those leering looks you think nobody notices—they also corrupt" (Matthew 5:28, The Message). Despite never having had an extra-marital affair, at least former President Jimmy Carter was honorable enough to admit his thoughts had at least wandered down the wrong path once or twice just as they have for every man except Jesus.

Billy's indiscretions were not just minor. In today's liberal culture we tend to excuse these kinds of bad behavior—especially when the perpetrator is someone who is likable or in a position of authority. We say such foolish things as, "it was just a little bit of flirting." There is no such thing as "innocent" flirtation.

Some will probably say the Church has had enough bad press, and we therefore should protect the congregation and God's name by not making a big fuss about it. Wrong, wrong, wrong. Sin is sin, and it is long past time that we say as much. Either a thing is true, or it is not—regardless of how we feel about it or how many times we have had to face it. Adultery, whether it is between the ears or between the sheets, is still adultery. One of the ministers who inspired me many years ago (thank you, Steve, for being such a man of God) once used a very good analogy. He said that if there were a bucket of nuclear material sitting in the middle of your living room you would not dance around it. You would run away from it as fast as you could.[9]

Why then do we men so often dance around the bucket of sexual temptation? Why do we think we can keep such things secret? Why do we think we can toy with such a dangerous thing and not be harmed? If we even remotely think we might get hurt, why do we neglect to consider that we harm everyone else around us by such behavior? We affect the lives of everyone around us by our failures in this area.

Some men try to excuse their flirtatious behavior by saying even more foolish things like, "I was just window shopping," or "I was just reading the menu." Men, that is not only wrong thinking, it is dangerous! When you think and say such things you are setting yourself up, and I dare say even planning to fail. Sex begins between your ears long before it happens between the sheets. When it comes to lust, do not go there. Instead of trying to dance with it, run from it! Lust is not just the physical act of adultery or sex. Flirting with women (or any other sort of lust) is inappropriate for any Christian, and particularly so for the Christian leader.

Many character flaws and mindsets will trip us up. The New Testament is loaded with very specific warnings about the things we should beware of if we wish to please our heavenly father and avoid falling down in our walk. Such things include: idolatry (having any other gods other than God), adultery (being married but having sexual intercourse with someone to whom you are not married, and I'll add that includes physical *and/or* emotional), fornication (not being married yet having sexual intercourse), drunkenness, witchcraft, legalism, not hearing God's Word (becoming "dull of hearing"), personal sloppiness, letting others deceive us, rejecting children, coveting, being overwhelmed in spirit, not looking out for the flock, taking God's grace lightly or presumptuously, abandoning sound Christian doctrine, giving up our commitment to Jesus, building up our lives improperly, causing others to trip, thinking we are infallible, getting caught up in meaningless arguments and unimportant matters, devouring each other, gossiping or lying about others, forgetting what we have learned in Christ, not fulfilling our ministry (service), being taken in by false doctrines, steadfastly refusing to accept the truth about God and our sinful nature because it does not agree with what we want to believe, rejecting prophecies concerning

Jesus, getting caught up in our own importance, loving to have others praise us, becoming wooden by following ceremony rather than the Holy Spirit, and accepting vain philosophies. Whew! And that list is not all-inclusive. I didn't just cook that up. Everything there is in the Bible. I think, though, that you get the idea. Read the list again. It can be a bit overwhelming. We are all guilty of at least a couple of those. This is why it is so easy for so many churches to become little self-promoting religious country clubs where nobody else is accepted.

The crux of the matter is that we stop seeking God. We stop desiring to hear what he has to say. We get lazy, and that trips us up big time. God's leaders—deacons, ministers, bishops, pastors, elders, overseers or whatever you wish to call them—must help the Church to grow in the middle of a "crooked and wicked generation [spiritually perverted and perverse]" (Philippians 2:15b). If these leaders do not stay on their toes and ensure they are not themselves falling into a trap, then they are doomed to fail. If they fail, their flocks also fail.

If we as Christians lose our ability to act as salt and light in this dark and fallen world, then how can any of us expect there to be any noticeable and beneficial difference between believers and unbelievers? I am sorry to say that in many churches today those proclaiming themselves Christians are worse examples of Christ than those who have nothing to do with the Church. True Christian leadership and respect begins with being an imitator of Jesus Christ, and once again that means sacrificing ourselves.

Throughout all of the ordeals at these churches, God repeatedly and consistently told me the same thing. It was only one word, "Stand." His command to me was to stand firm, to hold ground, to not run away or cave in. It was not easy. When the narcissistic pastor and his wife went off the deep end in their attempts to take over a church, God said, "Stand." When both pastor and elders refused to forgive and restore, God said, "Stand." When the spiritually immature elders became dull of hearing, when they had become incapable of receiving what God had to say, he said, "Stand." When the church's administrator began stealing huge sums of money from the very people whom he was supposed to take care of and took to sexually harassing my precious wife, God said, "Stand." After he finally released me from that place of almost unbelievable insanity and put me into a different congregation where the senior pastor floundered with his weakness for women, God said simply, "Stand."

One of the things I have traditionally had a hard time with is that I want to change people when they are behaving badly (including me). I wanted to change the pastor and his wife who tried to take control of one church. I wanted to change the board of elders who could no longer hear God's leading. I wanted to change the embezzler and sexual harasser, and I wanted to change the womanizing pastor.

I had to come to the point where I could accept that change belongs only to God. The problem is that even with all the right motives, no matter how much I may wish to I cannot change anyone in even the smallest of ways. God is the only one who can change any of us, and even then, we have to cooperate with him.

Here is the saddest part of all this insanity with churches that kill and wound the ones who need them most. Jesus spent much of his life here on earth seeking out the wounded. We should be doing the same, but we are not. We prefer to form our own little spiritual clubs where outsiders are not welcome unless they look and act just like us. If they don't dress like us or talk like us or come from the same economic status as us, then we look down on and judge the hurting instead of accepting, loving, restoring and healing them. Churches are supposed to be places of equipping Christians to serve others, not to be a "bless me club." Too many of us prefer to hole up in our church buildings and play at being holy.

So what should we do and not do? What kind of spiritual first aid can we bring to the wounded? To answer this I want us to look at the life of Job. Most Christians know this story, but just in case, here is the condensed version. Job led a successful, prosperous, and solidly grounded life in his reverence for God. God allowed Satan to test him, to try to make him give up on God. Then Job lost everything he had—his children, possessions and health—everything except for his life and a nagging wife who told him to curse God and die. Even his friends were not much help. They came to comfort him but instead wound up judging and condemning him. Does that sound like any of your church friends? When Job stopped complaining and began instead to pray for his friends, God gave Job twice what he had before his trials began.

The first thing to consider as spiritual first aid is to **bring comfort**. More often, many bring condemnation to those who are hurting. When we comfort another, we strengthen them and build them up. If we condemn them, we are judging, criticizing and tearing them down. That is not being helpful, and it is not what God tells us to do. If you read the book of Job, beginning in chapter four you will find the story of Job's friend, Eliphaz, giving him an earful.

In the first six verses, he essentially tells Job that because he (Job) had counseled so many people before he should take some of his own medicine. Basically, Eliphaz was saying, "Listen, Job. Because you have been so wise and godly all these years you ought to be able to take your own medicine by heeding the very advice you have given others about having a right relationship with God. Obviously you've done something wrong." I have to tell you, as a minister and a teacher it is one thing to have a pat answer, and it is altogether another thing to live it out.

Here is what I mean. When I have been at the lowest of lows in my life—when death, loss, or any major life calamity has taken me on—on more than one occasion I have not had the strength to do what I knew was right. I know that I am to love my wife, but when she was looking at me with daggers in her eyes and telling me that she wanted a divorce, doing what I knew to be right was not a simple matter. When I was out of work for a year and the bank was moving to foreclose on our house, I knew in my head that God is my provider, but I did not have the strength of mind and heart to believe it and walk in strong faith. Instead, I caved-in and wound up out in the front yard shaking my fist at the sky and screaming at God.

When someone is in this place, we need to avoid heaping condemnation on top of him or her or merely trying to advise them out of our own self-righteousness. That only makes things worse. The apostle Paul tells us in his letter to the Galatians that those who are trying to help others need to watch out. He said that if a person is misbehaving then those of us who are spiritual should set him or her straight, restore the person, and do so without getting proud of ourselves.[10]

If we are not careful, it becomes easy for us to become prideful, thinking we are better than the person who is in need. Not a one of us is free of flaws, weaknesses, wrongdoing or sin. Only the person who is perfect has a right to condemn us, and that person is God. Does he condemn us? Think hard before you answer.

My Bible says, "For God so greatly loved and dearly prized the world that he [even] gave up His only begotten (unique) Son, so that whoever believes in (trusts in, clings to, relies on) him shall not perish (come to destruction, be lost) but have eternal (everlasting) life. For God did not send the Son into the world in order to judge (to reject, to condemn, to pass sentence on) the world, but that the world might find salvation and be made safe and sound through Him" (John 3:16-17 AMP). The lesson for us is that is when we come across someone who is hurting or defeated we need to be a source of comfort and healing rather than of judgment and condemnation.

The second thing we need to do is to **keep our personal experiences to ourselves**. What I mean by that is that at different times God speaks to each of us, and a lot of what he shares with us is intended specifically just for us rather than for everyone else. In the story of Job, his friend Eliphaz comes and tries to comfort him by recounting a couple of his own personal experiences, thinking that in this situation what God had to say to him applied equally to Job.

The first lesson he tries to share with Job is the law of cause and effect. He shares a dream he had in which a voice asked him if a mortal can be more righteous than God can, if a man can be more pure than his maker. He tells Job that we sow what we reap. In essence, what he was saying to Job was that he was simply getting what he deserved. Cause: God is righteous and pure. Man is not. Effect: God is only giving you what you deserve as an unrighteous man. That's not very uplifting.

Eliphaz's intentions were probably for the good of Job. He was, after all, one of Job's closest friends. He was not aware, as we are now, of what preceded Job's losses. We know, but only because we have the first two chapters of Job which tell us Job's problems were not a result of his sin. Satan had accused God that the only reason anyone worships him is because of the blessings he gives them. God therefore allowed Satan to turn Job into a test case by removing God's blessings from Job's life.

The big mistake Eliphaz made here was in attempting to speak for God, based on his own experiences. If you understand what I have been saying so far you should know that God is perfectly capable of telling any person directly what he wants to say. The rest of us need to learn that, unless we are receiving very clear and specific instruction from the Spirit to the contrary, we should keep our personal experiences to ourselves. That is not to say that God doesn't use people to speak to us. He very often does; however, more often than not we simply spit out our own thoughts and opinions assuming their God's. That's dangerous!

The third act of spiritual first aid for us to render to the wounded is to *pick them up and carry them to Jesus.* In verses one through sixteen of chapter five, Eliphaz lectures Job about going to God. I hope that you are beginning to see that Eliphaz was not a good counselor. Job was so shaken to the core in his faith and confidence that the thought of going to God may not have even crossed his mind. People who are in such places of hurt and distress often cannot fend for themselves.

Here is a brief story to illustrate what I mean. I was born and raised in Hawaii, and one day when I was 17 and strong, I found myself a half-mile from shore in an undertow that was dragging out to sea. I fought and struggled, thrashing violently in the water. I began to believe I was going to die. I was afraid and in a panic. I knew I did not have the strength to swim all the way back to shore in that current. The more I struggled, the further from shore I went and the weaker I became. What I did not need at that point was someone coming along side of me in a boat shouting, "Swim! Come on! Swim harder! You can do it!" Telling someone who is hurting that he or she needs to pray more doesn't help. A person in a life-threatening predicament doesn't need counsel. He or she needs someone to help them.

There have been times in my life when I could not pray. I just did not have the strength to do so. In those places, I certainly did not need someone telling me to pray. What I needed was someone to pray for me.

Most of us who have spent any time in Sunday school, or listened to enough sermons, have heard at some point the story of the paralyzed man whose friends brought him to Jesus on a matt. The gospel of Matthew records an interesting response from Jesus in this story: "... and when Jesus saw *their faith*, he said to the paralyzed man, Take courage, son; your sins are forgiven and the penalty remitted" (Matthew 9:2b, my emphasis). He did not heal the paralytic because of that man's faith. He forgave and healed him because he saw the faith of his friends! When the man did not have the strength himself, they carried him to Jesus, believing Jesus would heal him.

Eliphaz told Job to go to God. That was the wrong response for the situation. We are the ones who should carry the wounded and hurting to Jesus, not tell them to take themselves to God. We must realize that often they do not have the ability to do so themselves. Imagine a soldier on the battlefield telling his wounded fellow soldier, "Man, you need to get up and get yourself to the hospital!" No, the good soldier sees his fallen comrade, picks him up and carries him to where he can receive the life sustaining help he needs, or brings that help to him. We need to be doing the same for those around us who we see are hurting and wounded.

We also need to *avoid saying foolish things* just because we like the sound of our own voices or because we feel we need to say something—anything—even if what we say is nothing more than meaningless dribble, tired old clichés that do nothing of any substance to help the one in need. Eliphaz did this. After first condemning Job, then improperly applying his own experiences to Job's life, followed by telling Job to seek God instead of praying for him, Eliphaz coughed up a phlegm of clichés, telling Job in verses seventeen through twenty-seven that God would use all of Job's sufferings to make him a better person.

I want to gag whenever I hear someone mistakenly say to one who is hurting, "Just hang in there. God is using this crisis in your life to make you a better person." While God can and does use the trials of our lives to chisel us, merely telling one who is hurting that the trial he or she is in is God's will does not comfort or help them. More often it hurts them more.

The other line that makes me sick is, "God will fix your problems if you just have more faith." In any given situation that may or may not be true. It is a matter between God and the individual. Who are we to determine whether or not another has faith? People who feel inadequate in their own faith think they have to dump condemnation on others by saying such empty things as "if you just have more faith." Those kinds of trite responses injure rather than heal.

God most certainly does heal and restore. In Job's case, that happened. You can read about it in chapter forty-two of Job. God healed him, restored his fortune and blessed him with twice what he had before. My point here—and one we do not like to admit—is that God is not obligated in any way to heal or restore. He does heal. He does restore, but not in every case. Many books out there will tell you God always heals, always restores. The reason there are so many books like that is not that God does always heal or always restore but because we like books with happy endings. Books with happy endings sell.

Here, however, is an example of the harsh reality of life. There was a woman who came to the church I attended years ago in New Hampshire. She had cancer. We prayed earnestly and repeatedly for her over many months, believing that God would heal her. She died from the cancer anyway. I honestly believe our pastor—a man for whom I have tremendous respect—had quite a battle with anger over that. When our problems get worse instead of better, and go on for years or even decades, most of us involved become angry or lose faith. Why? I think it is because for so long we have been spoon-fed the platitudinous lies that God will fix everything if we will only believe strongly enough.

A while ago my wife and I were discussing one of our own hardships. We had been facing some stressful financial issues. I felt she needed some encouragement and prayer. So I closed myself off in a room and prayed for her. Then I went to her, embraced her and said, "We'll get through this, honey."

She countered with "What if we don't? What if it just gets worse?"

I took a firmer stand. "We *will* get through this."

She retorted with, "What if we *don't*? What if God *doesn't* bring us out of all of this, but just allows it to go on?" She then brought up the example of Joni Eareckson Tada.

For those of you who do not know about Joni, when she was 17 she broke her neck in a diving accident. It left her a quadriplegic. Hospitalized for months, at one point she wanted to die. She prayed with all her heart repeatedly for God to heal her. Forty years later, she remains a quadriplegic. I could be wrong, but I think it is safe to say at this point that God is not going to heal her in this life. Could he? Absolutely! Will he? That is her story to tell.

It may make us feel better as we walk away from the hospital room of the cancer patient, or from the home of the chronically depressed wife or the widow struggling to live on a fixed income who misses her husband so much it hurts on top of her own physical pains, but our platitudes ("Don't worry, God will fix everything") are more often far more harmful than helpful.

Back in the book of Job, we find God scolding Eliphaz. He gives him a big black mark, saying, "… My wrath is kindled against you and against your two friends, for you have not spoken of Me the thing that is right, as My servant Job has" (Job 42:7). The lesson for us is that if all we can speak are clichés and platitudes then we need to keep our mouths shut.

Sometimes the best thing you can do for another who is hurting is not to hold out false hope or to recite meaningless clichés, but rather to just put your arm around them and cry *with* them. Do not condemn. Do not try to be God's mouthpiece. Do not offer your own experiences as lessons for them. Do not tell them to save themselves. Be real. Be compassionate. Be considerate. Carry them to God. Hurt with them. Trust God to be in control even when you cannot see the end of it.

In the middle of stressful news (I am leaving, and you cannot come with me), Jesus instructed his disciples, "Do not let your hearts be troubled (distressed, agitated). You believe in and adhere to and trust in and rely on God; believe in and adhere to and trust in and rely also on Me" (John 14:1). This was an imperative, a command. Trust is our gift back to God. In the middle of any crisis, our question always comes down to, "What do I really believe?" Instead of focusing on the immediate issue, we should focus on God and eternity. Our inclination is to ask God for the reason for our suffering. He rarely explains himself to us. Instead, he *reveals* himself to us and expects us to look ahead by considering our response. Trust is falling back into the arms of God even when we see him as small or weak.

Even though he had every right to, God did not condemn us. He identified with us. He did not just tell us what to do. He kept his promise to deliver us by sending his son to become fully God *and* fully man, in human skin, and experienced firsthand our pain and our suffering. He cried with us. He died for us. Who then are we to judge and condemn those who are hurting, broken, and worn down?

We have no right to reject the homosexual, the alcoholic, the drug addict, those who are not married yet living together and having sexual relations with each other, the adulterer, those who curse, those with tattoos or body piercings, those who do not dress the same as us, those who have less of an income or live in the "wrong" neighborhood, those of a different race, or even those who come from a different church or have a different take on some insignificant doctrine (e.g., make-up or no make-up, shorts or no shorts, and so on).

Jesus came and sought out those very kinds of people. He told the religious leaders of his day that he did not come to search for those who were well, but for those who were sick.

The Scribes and Pharisees, of course, did not understand. Many in the Church today still do not understand. Let me boil it down to one simple word: *compassion.* If you want forgiveness, you must forgive. If you want freedom from condemnation, then you need to be gracious, forgiving, and compassionate to those in need of healing and restoration. Do not kill or maim those whom God sends to you. Carry them. Comfort them. Forgive them. Encourage them. Build them up. Restore them. That, my friend, is why the Church is here. It is not to be a "bless me club." It is to be a place of healing, forgiveness and restoration for those in need. We have no excuse. One of the sayings of the church I attend to day is, "Touching disenchanted hearts with the heart of God." That is precisely the attitude for the Church.

THE GIFT OF FAITH

"Faith... is about struggle and having confidence precisely when the odds are the worst..."

Robert D. Kaplan[1]

Scripture tells us that without faith it is impossible to please God.[2] Therefore we would do well to find out as much as we can about faith and then to put that knowledge to use. Let us begin with a brief description.

We generally think of faith as a noun: belief, trust, hope and so on. Early on in my walk as a Christian, I came across the passage in Psalms in which the writer says, "VINDICATE ME, O Lord, for I have walked in my integrity; I have [expectantly] trusted in, leaned on, and relied on the Lord without wavering and I shall not slide" (Psalm 26:1 AMP). Initially I thought the writer was arrogant to say to God that he has been a man of integrity who has been unwavering, but my initial thoughts were wrong. I have since come to understand that this man was not saying he trusts in himself or his deeds. Instead, he is saying that his trust is in God and that his integrity is the visible outcome of that correctly placed trust or faith. I dare to say that we can think of faith as having the right attitude toward God, of putting our trust in the Lord rather than in self. Let us, therefore, look a little deeper into this issue of faith.

There is a story that has circulated for several years that goes something like this. A group of women in a Bible study were reading the book of Malachi. As they studied the third chapter, they came across verse three, which says, "He will sit as a refiner and purifier of silver, and he will purify the priests, the sons of Levi, and refine them like gold and silver, that they may offer to the Lord offerings in righteousness" (Malachi 3:3). The women found this verse a little confusing and wondered what it meant about the character and nature of God.

One of the women offered to find out about the process of refining silver and report back to the group at their next meeting. That week she called up a silversmith and made an appointment to watch him at work. She told him that she was curious about the process of refining silver, but she did not mention anything about her reason. As she watched, the silversmith held a piece of silver over the fire and let it heat up. He explained that in refining silver one must hold it in the middle of the fire where the flames are hottest in order to burn away all the impurities (dross).

The woman thought about God holding us in such a hot spot, then she thought again about the verse, that he "sits as a refiner and purifier of silver." She asked the silversmith if it was true that he had to sit there in front of the fire the whole time the silver was being refined. The man answered that yes, he not only had to sit there holding the silver, but he had to keep his eyes on it the entire time it was in the fire. If left in the flames even a moment too long the silver would be destroyed. (That gives me goose bumps!)

The woman was silent for a moment. Then she asked the silversmith, "How do you know when the silver is fully refined?"

He smiled at her and answered, "Oh, that's the easy part—when I see my reflection in it." Wow! Has God burned enough of my impurities away that he sees his reflection in me? Through the trials of our lives, God burns away the impurities in us so that we become a better reflection of him. He does not bring calamities upon us, but he does allow them in order to test our faith. Our part is to trust him when such trials come our way.

Now, I do not put much stock in stories that circulate on the Internet, but according to silversmith Fred Zweig[3] it is true. He said, "I am familiar with the verse from Malachi. The similarities of actual refining and the chapter and verse from the Bible are accurate. It is important not to overheat the silver when refined in this process, and clean molten silver will shine with a mirror-like quality when it is ready to pour. The high temperatures do volatize the impurities that form on the surface as dross. It is important to be attentive to the molten metal as it does it no good to overheat it. It may not destroy the silver, but silver has an affinity for absorbing oxygen and this can make it unworkable." I cannot speak for you, but I sure do not want God to consider me unworkable!

As I said a few moments ago, God permits the testing of our faith by trials. This is a hard thing for most of us to accept, but understand that he wants us to acquire patience and pliability. If we are constantly out of the fire of affliction, then we become stiff and useless. When Adam and Eve disobeyed God in Eden, we lost our divine shape, our divine image, and because of that, God wants to reshape us into his image. Little did I know when I first read this how it would soon strike home in such a personal way.

You might rightly assume that because I am a minister I have some knowledge of what comprises faith. As have many that call themselves Christians, it is a word I have heard most of my life. I have studied the meaning of faith in English, Hebrew and Greek. The New Testament uses the word as both an adjective and a verb.

To state it as simply as I can, faith is actively trusting God. Faith believes in, hopes in, and trusts in him rather than in self. Faith is coming to the point where you give up your own efforts to earn God's favor, and instead completely trust in Jesus alone as the means of salvation. Yet for all my exposure to this word, after all of my study and seeking, all I really had was head knowledge. There is a world of difference between what you know in your head and what happens when it drops that twelve or fourteen inches into your heart.

There is faith, and then there is faith. What I mean by that is that there are different kinds of faith. Because there are different meanings and interpretations, allow me to tell you up front of which I am speaking now—the *gift* of faith. Some describe it as a special ability God gives to certain people to see what God's will and promises are, to have great confidence in God, and then to act on his promises with unwavering belief in his ability to fulfill them. Faith is more than simply believing in God's ability. It both believes in his ability and that he will do what he has promised. While that is certainly true, I dare say that all faith is a gift from God.

Faith is a word with which most every Christian is familiar. In "church-speak" we "contend for the faith," are "saved by grace through faith," and "have faith in Jesus." So, is there any real difference in meaning in these uses of the word? Why would the apostle Paul, in his letter to the Corinthian church, list faith as a gift?[4] Dear reader, faith more than just believes something is true. Faith *acts* on belief.

Dr. Gene Scott—a pastor for over 50 years, the founding pastor of the Los Angeles University Cathedral and a widely recognized biblical languages expert—nailed it with his definition. He taught that faith is a verb—an action word, what we do. He said, "Faith is action, based upon belief, sustained by confidence in God's Word and his promise to perform it." He said a better word would be "faithing" because it indicates action rather than something static and lifeless.

I cannot think of a clearer way of putting it. If you have faith, then you act upon that faith because you believe God has both the ability and the will to do whatever he says he will do. There is a faith that saves you, faith that is a fruit of the Holy Spirit, and then there is the quite uncommon gift of faith.

I frequently struggle with my faith, and by that, I do not mean that I doubt my salvation through Jesus Christ. What

I mean is that I often struggle with letting go of my faith in me, and instead putting it fully in God. Most of us get impatient with God when he does not come through for us like a $20 bill from an ATM. When God does not seem to be doing what I think he should be doing, the way I think he should be doing it, and in the time frame in which I think it should be done; well, I tend to take matters into my own hands. Most all of us do this. Let's just admit it.

That is not faith in God. It is faith in self. For example, there have been many times I have struggled with the fact that with each passing month my bills seemed to grow larger and larger. Each payday I had to ask, "Okay, which of these bills must be paid right now, and which ones will just have to wait?" My flesh said, "You better get in gear and go find a second job in order to pay off those bills." That was trying to fix things with my own power, my own abilities. Whether I like it or not, it was simply my denial that God is big enough to keep his promises to me. I am not a slacker. I work hard and consistently give my employer more than is expected of me. I am neither a lazy man nor one who expects everything to be handed to me.

So then, why would God not keep his promise to provide for my needs? I am not saying here that getting a second job was out of the question, or that doing so would be evidence of a lack of faith on my part. What I am saying is that I was trying to fix the problem through my own efforts. If God wanted me to go get a second job, then that would be a different thing and I ought to be open to just such a possibility.

The part of me that wants me to be my own god tells me I need to be doing more. My spiritual side says I need to trust God instead. Now, if I just sat at home, did'nt want to work and simply complained about how God was not meeting my needs then I would be wrong, wrong, wrong—just as wrong as working hard but still not trusting God to take care of me.

I guess that is why God had the writers of the Bible put in all those wonderful examples of uncommon faith: Joseph, Moses, Gideon, Abraham, and so many others. Here are just a few examples of their faith. Keep in mind that all of these people were, as the writer of Hebrews put it, "still living by faith when they died. They did not receive the things promised; they only saw them and welcomed them from a distance ... they were longing for a better country—a heavenly one..." (Hebrews 11:13-16).

After Joseph recounted a few dreams in which he was in one way or another elevated above his brothers[5], they hated him, nearly murdered him, and then sold him into slavery. He was taken to Egypt where he was later unjustly accused of attempted rape and was put in prison where he sat for 20 years. His faith through all his trials shaped him into the man that God used to save the Hebrews from starvation after making Joseph second in Egypt only to the pharaoh.

Living in a time when it was common for raiding parties of Midianites, Amalekites and other eastern peoples to steal or destroy the Israelite's harvested crops and to kill every living thing, Gideon tried to hide while threshing his wheat harvest in a wine press. God sent an angel to him who called him "a mighty warrior."[6] Who would imagine a "mighty warrior" hiding in a wine press? Gideon tried to wriggle out of the commission by claiming that he was the weakest member of the weakest family. God won him over, and ultimately Gideon's faith made him precisely that. He raised an army of 32,000 men, then with God's leading reduced that to a mere 300. With them he went into battle against the combined army of the Midianites, Amalekites and others, and soundly defeated them.

Despite growing up as an adopted son of the pharaoh, Moses' faith took him to where he chose to disassociate from his Egyptian family and instead receive the mistreatment of the Egyptians as a Hebrew. Because of his faith, God was able to use Moses to lead the Hebrews out of Egypt in a miraculous way.[7]

Abraham became the epitome of faith. God told him to leave his family and his country and go to a place that he would show him (Genesis 12:1). God didn't even tell him up front where that would be. In essence he simply said, "I am not telling where now. Just go. I will show you the way later." Abraham obeyed.

He begged God for a son, and then believed him for that son for decades, even though both he and his wife were well past the age of bearing children. (They were in their 90s when God promised him a son.) What came about from Abraham's faith in God for a son was the Israelite nation. Them, to test Abraham's faith, when his son Isaac was a young man, God told him to sacrifice this only son. I do not know if I could even contemplate such a thing, but Abraham had such trust in God that he believed God always had his best interests in mind. At the moment that

Abraham raised his knife over his son Isaac on the altar, God stayed his hand.[8]

The examples of men of faith in the Bible, all of whom were flawed in many ways, may also be why I like David's psalms so much. In addition to his songs of praise and worship of God, he boldly and unashamedly voiced his cares and struggles with his faith. He cried out to God. He blamed God. He confessed his lost confidence in God. Despite all of his failures in trusting God, God loved him and called him a man after his own heart.[9] Now why would he say something like that about a man who so often failed? I think it is simply because whenever he fell, David got back up and returned to seek God's heart. God did not expect David to be perfect, but he was delighted that David loved him.

Many of us have heard evangelical ministers tell us to "just believe," or something to the effect that we just have to take "a blind leap of faith." It is not my intention to put them down because, for the record, there are indeed times when God will ask you do to something that goes completely contrary to common sense. For example, Oswald Chambers—one of my favorite devotional writers—said, "Jesus Christ demands of the man who trusts him the same reckless sporting spirit that the natural man exhibits. If a man is going to do anything worthwhile, there are times when he has to risk everything on his leap, and in the spiritual domain Jesus Christ demands that you risk everything you hold by common sense and leap into what he says, and immediately you do, you will find that what he says fits on as solidly as common sense."[10] It is my experience that, while those occasions do arise now and then, they are the exception rather than the norm.

In their attempts to get people to accept Jesus Christ as their Lord, some well-intentioned Christians take shortcuts by urging people to set aside all reason and "just believe." While such an approach may get a person to make a confession of faith in Jesus, eventually he or she will still have to come to a point where they fully understand why they believe. There are enough Scripture passages that speak about believing with our mind that I am convinced God expects us to generally use our brains as part of our faith. (Which does not mean that he never expects us to set reasoning aside.) We cannot shoehorn God into our preconceived notions of either his character or ways. He does everything to perfection with his will, not ours. He does not cut corners. He challenges us to test and prove him, and he gives us solid reasons and evidence to believe in him.

Contrary to some popular teaching, faith is not blind. God will certainly ask us to do things we do not understand, but here is the critical point: our faith does not lie in our understanding a particular issue. It is, instead, grounded in an understanding of the person and character of God. We do not muster up faith by gritting our teeth and determining that no matter how much we may not believe at the moment that we will somehow force ourselves to believe anyway. Come on. We do not even fool ourselves when we do that, and we are certainly not making a good impression on God. He does, after all, know every thought of our hearts and sees everything that we do. He knows if we truly believe or not, so pretending to believe when we really don't is nothing more than a lie; and a weak one at that. We do not fool anyone but ourselves when we do such a thing, and more often than not we do not even fool ourselves.

Faith is not a warm, fuzzy feeling. Looking at my pile of bills I am not thinking, "It doesn't matter if I don't have the money in the bank to pay these." However, I am trusting God to help me pay them because I know he cannot go back on his word and that he has promised to care for my needs.[11] He does not promise to meet all my selfish desires but he does promise to take care of my needs (and he also says he wants to bless me with the desires of my heart ... just not so much the selfish ones).

Faith is not the result of our own works. We do not become religious enough for "real faith" to kick in and transform us into "Super Christians." We do not suddenly reach this invisible point where we can push the Nitrous-Oxide faith button on our religious super-chargers and scream through to the finish line.

It is not about fighting and struggling to keep on believing. While we will indeed struggle from time to time, that is still trying to make it by our own efforts. How often we go to church, how much we study the Bible, how many times or how fervently we pray, how much we give in time or money—none of it makes one iota of difference in the matter of pleasing God. He looks first at our hearts.

Unless our hearts desire him first and fully, then all we may do is meaningless. The things we do—the Bible calls them "works"—will follow us if we do have faith, but that faith comes before the doing. Faith is not clinging to hope or some particular belief. It is holding on to God and trusting him because we know he is true to his character and word.

Let me give you a hypothetical example of what I mean. This example is really more about trust than faith, but it should get you thinking in the right direction. If I asked you why you go to your particular dentist, what would you say? More than likely it would be something about how he or she was in the top ten percent of his or her class in dental school, or because you have been seeing this dentist for years and you have always had good experiences. It may even be because a trusted friend or someone in your family recommended him or her to you. I seriously doubt you would say you trust your dentist based on nothing more than force of will. You placed faith in your dentist because of personal or related knowledge. In other words, your faith in your dentist is based on something—it is not blindly based on nothing other than raw determination.

I have faith that when I ask my children a question they will answer with the truth. That is not blind faith. I have taught them and observed them over the years, and with few exceptions they have always told me the truth. I know them better than just about anyone else, and sometimes even better than they know themselves. My faith in their honesty is based on a relational knowledge of them. It is not blind.

The same is true of faith with and in God. It is based on a relationship with him, on some knowledge, some rational expectation. It is vital to understand this because it makes the gift of faith all the more amazing. God does not ask us to check our brains at the door. In fact, he challenges us to test him. The psalmist tells us to taste and see that the Lord is good,[12] while the prophet Malachi says God challenges us to prove him.[13] You see, our testing or proving God strengthens our faith in him.

For many years I had often read and heard quoted the scripture that says, "I am crucified with Christ: nevertheless I live; yet not I, but Christ liveth in me: and the life which I now live in the flesh I live by the faith of the Son of God, who loved me and gave himself for me" (Galatians 2:20 KJV). I emphasized the word "of" there because the King James Version translators got that one right where others have incorrectly translated the word as "in." The faith of which the apostle Paul speaks in that passage is not *in* the Son of God; it is the faith *of* the Son of God himself. In other words, it was *Christ's* faith that saved me. It was not *my* faith. In fact, I was not even consciously looking for God. It was actually quite the opposite case: he was looking for me. This is one of the significant distinguishing differences between Christianity and all other religions of the world: God came looking for us!

God put the faith into me that brought me to the point of believing. The apostle Paul tells us that it is God who gifts us with faith and that this faith is his unmerited favor (grace).[14] Unfortunately, many believe that the faith needed for salvation is something that comes from within us. It does not. God gifts us with this kind of faith as well.

The matter of the gift of faith and Paul's phrase, "the degree of faith," (or "measure of faith" in the King James Version) was brought home to me in a very personal way a few years ago. Before I begin the story allow me to say that my daughter, now an adult, gave me permission to tell it. My wife and I had gone out on one of our rare "date nights," leaving our youngest child—16 years old at the time—at home by herself. Not a big deal. When we got home she made a minor complaint about a stomachache, and then retired to her room where at that age she spent most of her time. I thought nothing more of it, and went about my normal routine of getting into my pajamas, watching a bit of the nightly news on television, letting dogs out for the last time of the evening, turning lights off, securing doors, and so on.

As I was dozing off I heard a muffled cry through the adjoining wall of our bedrooms. It was so faint that it barely registered in my already half-asleep mind. A few moments later I heard it again. It was not the cry of someone who is sad. Instinctively I knew something was seriously wrong. I jumped out of bed and ran to her door only to discover it was locked. I knocked on her door and called out, but there was no answer—not even the sound of movement within her room. I began to panic. I jiggled the doorknob; perhaps thinking that doing so might unlock the door or at least make her realize I wanted to come in to find out what was going on. Still there was no response. Then I began shouting and pounding on the door, waking everyone in the house. Desperation was taking hold. Not exactly the picture of faith.

With my wife now at my side, our daughter finally unlocked the door, crying in heaving sobs. For some reason I knew this was more than hormonal or teenage emotional upset. She was scared to death, and obviously very much in serious trouble.

We tried to get her to tell us what was going on, but she refused to confide in us, only crying instead. I became firm, telling her it was not a game, and that she needed to tell us what was the matter. As it would be with any loving parent, my immediate and primary concern was for her wellbeing. After a few minutes of utter fear, our daughter decided to tell us what was going on. Through her panicked cries she told us that while we were out she had decided in her naiveté to find out what it feels like to get high, and consequently had taken numerous pain pills—at least a couple of anything she could find in the house— aspirin, Ibuprofen, Tylenol, even liquid cold and flu medicines. She had taken a little of anything she could lay her hands on.

I don't think I have ever changed out of pajamas and into jeans and a t-shirt as quickly as I did that night. I virtually jumped out of them and into street clothes. My wife and I raced her to the nearest hospital where we spent the remainder of the night.

Much to my relief the hospital staff decided that rather than pumping her stomach the best course of action was to intravenously put as much liquid into her as they could, and sent me home to find as many of the medicine containers around the house as I could. While nurses started an IV on her, I jetted home, gathered up everything that she might have taken, and returned to the hospital with bag in hand.

Upon my return they meticulously went through everything in the bag with our daughter, one item at a time. "Did you take this? How much? Did you take any of these? No? Okay, how about these? How many?" And so it went until they had grilled her about each and every medicine. Even though she had not done so, they thought she had attempted a suicide and informed us that, according to state law she had to be admitted to a psychiatric institution. She never was admitted—there were no beds available—and for that I am grateful. After the experiences with my sister's state hospital stays I just do not have much faith in state-mandated programs.

God answered my prayers that night. Our daughter came home with us the following morning having learned quite a lesson, and other than being tired and shook-up she was okay. She had rightfully been in fear for her life. The doctor told me that if she had taken just a couple more of the pills she would have been in a life-threatening situation.

So, you ask, what does that have to do with faith and in particular with faith being a gift? After all, it doesn't sound like I was exhibiting faith in any sort of biblical proportion. It was most assuredly a scary situation for all of us—one I neither anticipated nor expected. It would have been completely understandable to panic, fearing the worst possible outcome. That kind of reaction would be the normal, natural response of a parent over a child in very serious medical trouble. But I did not come unglued. Why not?

There was a time many years before this episode when a candle sitting on our wood stove melted and caught fire, spreading over the stove. I was comically trapped between the kitchen and the living room, moving first toward the living room, then back to the kitchen, then to the living room and then back to the kitchen. I knew what to do but just could not get my brain and body to work together. I was in a state of panic. Then my wife handed me the baking powder and told me to put it on the flames. Shake, shake, flames out. It is good to have someone at peace nearby when you are panicking!

Why didn't I lose it in this far more perilous situation with my daughter? The best way I can describe it is that it was because God placed into me that night—for that specific situation—the gift of faith. The faith I had that night was not the result of prayer, or Bible study, or even of being as some would say religious—being saved, going to church, reading the Bible—or even of being a minister. GOD placed faith into me that night, or maybe he simply activated the faith he had already placed there.

I don't know exactly what happened, but what I do know is that I didn't work it up, and I certainly hadn't earned it. I did not mindfully force myself to believe that God was in control. It was a kind of faith I had never experienced before. It just suddenly flicked on like a light switch. It was a freely given gift. Without even thinking about it, I trusted him completely with my daughter. It had nothing to do with my knowledge, my abilities, my righteousness, or even my asking. I did not ask: there wasn't time. True to the words of Jesus, God knew what I needed even before I could ask. It was a gift, and I accepted it without a moment's hesitation.

Was I happy about what was going on with my daughter? Absolutely not. Was I concerned? You bet I was!

Was I saying—as some religious people might say I should have—"Thank you, God, for allowing my daughter to seriously threaten her own life with these pills because I just know somehow you're going to bless this?" No way. How phony that would have been. Was I afraid? No, I wasn't, but only because God had put his faith into my heart that night. That in turn enabled me to trust him completely with the care of my daughter. That is the "gift of faith."

I believe God will give this gift to any of us in times of need if we will only accept it. What I want you to see is that, as with any gift, we cannot possess it until we first accept it. In order to accomplish his will, God will put such faith into those who will accept it.

The one, who like the apostle Peter, can say to the lame, "rise up and walk,"[15] does so only because God put that faith into him or her. Miracles do not happen because a person has become holy enough to do such works. Peter, walking on the water to Jesus on the Sea of Galilee, did so not because of his faith. It was the gift of faith that God had put into him. The moment he took his eyes off of Jesus and put them back onto the waves, he began to sink. Of course it was not his faith that enabled him to walk on water. Likewise, it was not my faith that kept me at peace while my daughter was in trouble. It was God's faith with which he had gifted me that night that kept me sane and at peace.

Unfortunately, some "miracles" are choreographed fakeries. Yes folks, it's true, and this minister is calling it out. Some miracles are simply made to appear genuine by either, or both the person receiving the miracle or the one praying for them. And some alleged miracles happen because of the power of the mind. It is not all that uncommon for psychosomatic illnesses—which can have true physical manifestations—to be cured by the power of suggestion. The person stops believing he or she has a malady, and so the symptoms disappear.

Real miracles, I believe, happen because it is God's will for them to happen, and because he has those there who will accept and make use of his gift of faith. Because they are willing to allow God to place into them utmost confidence in his ability, he is then able through the faith within them—faith he placed there—to perform the miracle. This is what I believe happened when Peter told the lame man to "rise up and walk." Peter exercised the faith with which God had gifted him, and the result was the miracle of a lame man walking and leaping. It was neither Peter's nor the lame man's faith that caused him to walk. It was Peter's use of the gift of faith from God that did so. God performed the miracle. God certainly is not limited to working through people, but I am convinced that he chooses to do so more often than not.

Another aspect of faith that God has shown me is that faith is not about you—and especially not about you being holy or religious enough to have it. It is based on something tangible, something you can see—whether that is with your eyes, your head, your heart or your spirit. It is not blind. I have faith in God because the evidence for his existence is overwhelming. Did you catch that? Evidence—what one must use in court to prove or disprove a case.

God does not ask us to check our brains at the door. Instead, as I said earlier, he challenges us to test him, to prove him, to taste of his goodness. The author of the book of Hebrews tells us that if we do not have faith then it is impossible to please God. He says that if we are going to come to God we must—by necessity—believe that he rewards those who diligently seek him.[16] That kind of belief is not something we just drum up from within ourselves. It comes from God, and it comes from our weighing the evidence and coming to the conclusion that God is indeed who he claims to be.

I think it takes more faith—in the way most think of faith as a blind leap in the dark—to not believe in God. There just is not any evidence at all to support the contention that God does not exist. One has to really want to believe he doesn't exist, and completely ignore all the evidence to the contrary in order to keep that mindset. If you set out to disprove the existence of God, but keep an open mind in the process, then I believe you will come away convinced that he does exist. Just ask people like C.S. Lewis[17] and Lee Strobel.[18] The evidence is simply overwhelming. To believe otherwise one must reject all evidence of God's existence.

When I tell someone I have faith that God is going to intercede for them in a given situation (and I do not do that either lightly or indiscriminately), it is not merely a matter of my wanting to believe for the best. It is because I have already seen God intervene in similar situations for similar reasons, and because I know what God says about it in the Bible. Yes, just like the Sunday-School song, "Jesus loves me this I know for the Bible tells me so…"

In the famous chapter on faith (chapter 11), the writer of the book of Hebrews said that faith is the assurance, the confirmation of what we hope for, that it is the proof of what we do not see, that it is a conviction born out of what we know even if we do not detect it with our senses.[19] Faith—which goes hand-in-hand with hope—is a firm persuasion.

This is foundational. This kind of faith is what you can build your life upon. It is no whim or momentary decision to believe something regardless of all evidence to the contrary. That is not to say that a person who makes an emotional decision to follow Jesus does not have faith, but it must be accompanied by, or be quickly followed by faith based on evidence. Even when problems arise, and continue, this kind of faith is a conviction that remains.

The apostle John states in his gospel, written primarily to non-Christians, that the reason for his writing was "that you may believe."[20] He presented evidence to persuade and convince. He was not saying, just believe, regardless. He was saying here is the evidence so that you *will* believe. In his other letters, written to Christians, he stated that his purpose in writing to them was "so that you may know [with settled and absolute knowledge]."[21] There's a big difference there!

True faith can, and will be shaken, but it will never be broken. I will attest to that from personal experiences. The object of our faith (God) must exit. There is no other real possibility. It is proved to be. Faith provides a reality—or as the writer of Hebrews put it, substance—to that for which we hope. Noted Bible scholar Kenneth Wuest[22] said it this way, "Faith apprehends as a real fact what is not revealed to the senses. It rests on that fact, acts upon it, and is upheld by it in the face of all that seems to contradict it. Faith is real seeing."[23] The late world renowned Greek translator, Spiros Zodhiates,[24] said the meaning of the word "faith" as used in Hebrews 11:1 is "that persuasion is not the outcome of imagination but is based on fact, such as the reality of the resurrection of Christ, and as such it becomes the basis of realistic hope."[25]

Here is an example of the contrast between faith in what is not seen and facts. The analogy is not perfect, but it will give you an idea of what I mean when I say that faith is based on something objective. Let us assume you know me. Imagine I am standing in front of you. I put my right hand into my pocket, and as I do so you hear the jingle of a few coins—not an uncommon occurrence.

I pull my hand out of my pocket in a fist and say to you, "I have a coin in my hand. Do you believe me?" Most likely you would say, "Sure, I believe you." You have no reason to believe otherwise. I have not lied to you before, and anyway why would I lie about such an insignificant thing? You did, after all, hear the change in my pocket as I put my hand into it. Your response is a statement of faith. You have faith that I am telling you the truth because of what you know of me and because your senses told you that there was a high probability that I was being truthful.

Now I say more specifically, "I have a quarter in my hand. Do you still believe me?" Again, you most likely would answer in the affirmative. You know, as do I, that when I reach into my pocket to get a coin I can easily determine the difference between a penny, a nickel, a dime and a quarter. I do not have to see it to fasten my hand on the right coin or to know what is in my hand. It has a knurled edge, and is a certain size and weight. Almost anyone can pull the right coin out of a pocket when trying to get a quarter. So you still have justifiable reason for such faith. Without first seeing them you have pulled quarters out of your pockets too.

"Now," I say to you, "I am going to destroy your faith," and I open my hand to reveal the coin. You see the quarter there. What you have is no longer faith. It is an observation of fact. That is the difference between faith and observable fact.

This is why the author of the book of Hebrews wrote, "Now faith is the substance of things hoped for, the evidence of things not seen." We who believe that Jesus is the Christ have faith, and that faith is not unreasoned. If we try to drum up faith where there is no reason for firm conviction, then it is not faith at all. It is only wishful thinking. One day we will see him face-to-face, and then we will no longer have need of faith. In the meantime we must go through life here on earth, trusting and being firmly convinced of the truth, convinced because we have relational, experiential knowledge of the one who is in control.

Our own reason plays a significant role in our faith walk, but it is not only our minds that make such a life possible. If it were, then there would be no need for faith. God gifts us with faith, and with our minds we respond to him, turning from our own ways and trusting him. This turning, this repentance as we Christians call it, goes beyond our own reason and logic. Dr. Ronald E. Cottle,

president of Beacon University, says that "My faith is …
beyond my reason … It is not irrational, but transitional.
My faith informs my reason, and my reason faithfully
questions my faith, not to deter it, but to keep it clear and
focused."[26]

Question 21 of the Heidelberg Catechism asks, "What is
true faith?" The correct response is, "True faith is a sure
knowledge whereby I accept as true all that God has
revealed to us in His Word. At the same time it is a firm
confidence that not only to others, but also to me, God has
granted forgiveness of sins, everlasting righteousness, and
salvation, out of mere grace, only for the sake of Christ's
merits. This faith the Holy Spirit works in my heart by the
gospel."[27]

We must then ask the question, "From where does faith
come?" The apostle Paul said in his letter to Christians in
Rome that faith comes by hearing.[28] Bible scholar and noted
commentator Albert Barnes[29] said, "When it is said that
faith cometh by hearing, it is not meant that all who hear
actually believe, for that is not true; but that faith does not
exist unless there is a message, or report, to be heard or
believed. It cannot come otherwise than by such a message;
in other words, unless there is something made known to
be believed. And this shows us at once the importance of
the message, and the fact that people are converted by the
instrumentality of truth, and of truth only." What message?
The answer is simple: the gospel (good news) of Jesus
Christ. Once again, this gift of faith comes not from us but
from God.

Faith is not something we create within ourselves out of nothing. While we are instructed to increase in our faith (to grow in it),[30] we do not create faith in any capacity. In fact, even the little faith any of us have is God's gift to us. This does not mean we are nothing more than puppets.

There is a very important distinction between free will and predestination. Both have been highly debated by theologians, and religious leaders through the centuries. To put it as simply as I can, predestination is the thinking that even before the world existed God chose those whom he desired to be saved. That much is biblical, and I have no issue with it. What I do object to is the underlying idea that those he chose have no option. It is their destiny. God decreed it, and therefore it will happen. The individual's decision is more than mere probability, it is a predictive outcome.

Free will, on the other hand, is the concept that believes that even though God knows beforehand the outcome of each and every decision everyone ever makes, he allows us to make our own decision. I think that makes much more sense and still gives God credit for being omnipotent and omniscient (all-powerful and all-knowing).

You see it is God who gives us every bit of faith we have. In fact, as I said a minute ago, the Bible tells us that what faith we have is the result of hearing the Word.[31] That much sides well with predestination. However, I believe that once God gives us this faith to believe in Jesus, we then have the choice to act upon that gift of faith. This falls into the free will side. God does not pull the strings of faith, leaving us with no other option than to respond to him as he wishes.

Just read the Old Testament if you do not think that is true. His chosen people consistently wandered off on their own. Did God make them do that? No! Neither does he make us merely passive recipients of his grace. Our part always has been, and always will be, to believe him, to trust him, to have a firm conviction and to act upon it.

Speaking of faith in his book "From Rebellion to Redemption," Christian author and Fuller Theological Seminary graduate Randall Working said the following.

> Faith is more than just a warmth in my heart. It is more than just feeling good about God's love for me. There is content to the Christian faith. To be a Christian is to be sorry for the wrong I've done and to turn away from it; it is to trust in the work of Jesus dying in my place; and it is to commit myself to living for him ... The most important thing about faith is not the amount of faith, but the object of one's faith ... persons we perceive as having "great faith" are usually people who've discovered it's not about their faith at all. They are often people who are actually aware of their own weakness and their utter dependence on Christ ... People of great spiritual power are people who know they need God ... you don't need great faith. But you do need faith in the One who can do great things.[32]

So then, faith is neither about me or you, nor about our doing anything of great importance to create faith within us. Before we come to this place of trust, of faith, we must first come to the point of recognizing our great need of the Savior. We don't like to do that. We would rather make excuses. Here then is one of the most important lessons I have learned in my trials: faith is all about *God's gift to me*, and of *my response to him*. It is about recognizing my need of him, and of learning experientially of his absolutely unchanging character. If there is true intimacy between God and me; then when he speaks, I will hear and respond in faith and love, believing and trusting that he will do all he has promised. That, my friend, is the gift of faith.

Chiseled by Trial

STAYING IN THE ZONE

The soul is dyed the color of its thoughts. Think only on those things that are in line with your principles and can bear the full light of day. The content of your character is your choice. Day by day, what you choose, what you think, and what you do is who you become. Your integrity is your destiny...
It is the light that guides your way.

Heraclitus
Greek Poet, Philosopher

The core of Christian living is learning to walk with the Lord, day in and day out, remaining consistent in attitude and behavior despite life's circumstances. That is not always a simple task. I believe God desires for the painful places through which we must go to prepare us for the heights to which he wishes to take us. He does not heal us, or make us complete simply for us to go on with life as before, or even to live life as we wish to have it. God does these things in order to use us for his purposes. That is what ministry is all about. Ministry is not the exclusive realm or responsibility of ministers or even church staffs. It is about all of us serving others. Christ commands us, "Go then ..."[1] serving people. When he discerned that his disciples were talking among themselves about who was the best he called them together and said, "If anyone desires to be first, he must be last of all, and servant of all."[2] It just does not get any clearer than that.

Many of us think a do-as-you-like or unencumbered divine blessing is itself the highest reward one can experience in life, and yet most don't regularly enjoy such blessing, which begs the question, "Why not?" Divine blessing comes from taking as much advantage of Scripture as possible. It does not consist in a lack of problems, nor is prosperity necessarily a result or indicator of God's blessing on one's life. There are a lot of very ungodly people who are materially very well off, so forget using that as the determining factor.

Go grab a Bible and open it up to Psalm 119. The first eight verses address this topic of how we should live and the importance of staying on the right path. It begins with an exclamation of how blessed people are who stay on the right path. It is interesting to note the meaning of the word "blessed" as it is used there. It comes from the Hebrew word which means to go straight, to walk on, to advance, to make progress.[3] Another significant meaning of the word is "happiness."[4] So a blessed or happy person is one who is walking straight, advancing and making progress.

To give you an example of what I mean by that, I watched this very thing occur when my youngest daughter was a junior in high school. She decided she wanted to join the girls' lacrosse team. It was only the second year her school had ever played because it was only the second year of the school's existence. In just a few short months, her team went from a disorganized group of novices to becoming the number two team in the state. They worked hard, which in turn resulted in a visible improvement in their skills. They made progress, and because they could see that progress, they became pleased and happy with themselves. That feeling in turn fueled their desire to keep playing and getting better, which resulted in getting good enough at the game to almost win the state finals. They missed first place by only one point in the final match.

In verse one of Psalm 119, however, a game is not being played. The writer is speaking of a way of life. A blessed or happy person is walking an undefiled life for the Lord. Most in our Western society today have difficulty with the word "undefiled." We think it means there cannot be anything wrong with us; we must be spotless, perfect. However, the literal meaning is "complete."[5]

In this same verse in the KJV, we find the word "law."[6] The Hebrew word for law is "torah," which means instruction, particularly from the Pentateuch—the first five books of the Bible: Genesis, Exodus, Leviticus, Numbers and Deuteronomy. God gave these guidelines to us for covenant relationship with him. Jewish commentators write that torah literally means "teaching" or "direction," and indicates a legal system—the whole will of God imparted to man for guidance. We cannot keep the whole law perfectly, and so we need Jesus. If our way of life is in Jesus, who fulfilled all the law, then we are blessed or happy people—literally complete and whole.

In the second verse of Psalm 119, the psalmist declares, "Blessed (happy, fortunate, to be envied) are they who keep his testimonies, and who seek, inquire for and of him and crave him with the whole heart." The word "testimonies" there are his affirmations—his testimony as in a court of law—of what in our relationship with God is right and wrong.[7] This verse tells us that a happy person keeps God's testimonies.

How do we do that? For starters, we do not give it away. We do not lose it. The word "keep" here has an even deeper meaning. The word literally means to guard or to watch over[8] as would a military sentry. A happy Christian, a blessed Christian, watches over and guards the testimonies of the Lord.

That does not mean we hoard them so nobody can take them away from us. While we of course do not want to lose or misplace the knowledge that the Lord has spoken for truth and against sin, to guard over these truths in a sense where we do not want to share them with anyone else is not only wrong thinking it is unscriptural. We are to be a testimony, a living witness for the Lord. We are to reflect the glory of God like Moses did when he came down off Mt. Sinai with his face shining so brightly that others could not look at him until he put a piece of cloth over his face. We are to guard against the evil one and the temptation to throw away the truth, but we are also to share God's glory with everyone.

To keep the Lord's testimony of truth in your heart, you must seek him with all your being. Jesus, teaching from the torah, instructed us to "… love the Lord your God with all your heart and with all your soul and with all your mind (intellect)" (Matthew 22:37).

Your heart is your innermost being. Your soul is your mind, will and emotions together. Your mind is your intellect and reasoning abilities. We must seek him with all of our being. To seek indicates a repeated motion—continuously coming back—to read and meditate on Scripture repeatedly.[9] Have you ever lost your car keys or the remote control for your television? You went seeking for it, and if you are at all like me I bet you went back and looked in a few of the same places more than once ... like maybe under the couch seat cushions. That is what it means to seek. We are to progress beyond just memorizing a few verses of God's Word, to exploring it diligently and repeatedly so that we come to fully comprehend the truth.

Searching God's truth also helps us to discover the sins in our own lives. Most of us don't like that, but it *is* necessary. In the next chapter I write about how you have to be crushed in order to be set apart for God's use. Becoming holy or set apart requires surrendering your will and instead yielding to God's. That includes recognizing *your* sin instead of focusing on others, admitting and confessing it by calling it sin instead of something lesser, and repenting of it, which means to turn away from it with remorse. There won't be any pleas of "not guilty" or "no contest" in Heaven before the throne of God.

Coming back to that word "testimonies" again, the word translated in the KJV comes from the Hebrew word for "witness" or "testimony," but it also stems from that which is round or repeated.[10] Like a wedding ring, it is symbolic of constancy. In our context here of right living before God, it consists of the things that witness to the enduring quality of God's covenant—the tabernacle, the ark and its contents, but especially the Ten Commandments.

In the New Testament, this word connects with backing up the truth of the Gospel through our lives. It is walking the walk, not just talking the talk. The famous 19th century Bible commentator, Albert Barnes said, "Every law of God is his solemn testimony of what is right and good."[11] Therefore, a happy person is one who is making progress, walking with Jesus; one who guards God's instructions concerning right and wrong conduct, returning constantly to the Word as his teacher.

The happy people of Psalm 119 do nothing wrong. Do you know anyone who does nothing wrong? I didn't think so. Me neither. What the phrase, "do nothing wrong" means is that you do nothing that is the opposite of God's character or opposite that of righteousness.[12] It does not mean that you never ever sin, but that it is your habitual, characteristic practice to avoid wrong thoughts, words and actions. This should be your normal style of living.[13]

To understand what this means, think of the bug in the animated film, "A Bug's Life."[14] In one scene a moth, attracted by the light of a bug zapper, is unable to resist flying into it because, as the moth cried out on its crash course to death, "… it's soooooo beautiful." It was the bug's nature, its character and its habit to fly toward the light. It should be our nature, our habit, to avoid that which is wrong and to seek to do God's will.

These blessed or happy people of Psalm 119 "walk in his ways." Another way of putting that is to "go the distance" or "take a journey."[15] These people are in it—this thing we call the Christian life—for the long haul. Our walk is no short trip. We are here for eternity. Most of us in our microwave age have a hard time remembering that.

If you want to live a happy Christian life, if you want blessings along the way, then take the road that the Lord has already mapped out for you. Seek his leading instead of your own. If you try to figure it out for yourself, you will only get lost. I don't know about you, but when I get lost I become frustrated, sometimes even panicky. Instead, let the Lord be your strength, your beacon of light. He will guide you and show you how to get "from here to eternity."

Be careful to interpret that correctly. These ways are neither about getting as close to the edge as possible, nor about a path we manage to step onto occasionally. We cannot be Sunday morning Christians. These ways are where we habitually and characteristically walk. This means avoiding behaviors and thoughts we know will lead us away from God. We are always watching him, taking our cues from him, and mimicking his ways.[16]

To walk in this way you must accept the authority of the Word of God and the authority of the voice of the Spirit of God. The word used in verse four is "ordained," meaning, "commanded."[17] That's a strong word!

This is one of the great differences between Christianity and the secular humanism that seems to rule American culture today. We Christians do not do things because we judge them according to our individual standards be beneficial to us. That is relativism. We do what we do because we believe in a God who holds ultimate authority over us. If we do not believe this about God, we miss the boat. We cease to be his people. When we do not believe God is the ultimate seat of all authority then we have returned to worship of self, which in turn separates us from the one true God.

In verse four of this psalm, the writer says that God has ordered us to keep his precepts. The word "precept"—from the root meaning "of a visit"[18]—is a principle instructing specific and certain action that must be obeyed by all who are part of the contract or covenant.[19] It is the responsibility of specific actions that God gives us as his people. In other words, God's precepts are his instructions to us of what we as his covenant people are to do—how we are to live. They are not suggestions.

Here is an example of what I mean. If you have read the chapter on suffering injustice, then you already know that I was unjustly charged with felony reckless endangerment with a deadly weapon. Because I had never even had so much as a parking ticket, and rather than taking it to a grand jury trail, the court agreed to grant me a pre-trial diversion which put me on probation for a year and a half. That was a legally binding contractual agreement, or covenant. It came with very specific conditions.

Among those conditions, I had to report to a probation officer every month. I could not own a firearm. I could not enter a liquor store. I could not even leave the county without written permission. If I received even so much as a traffic ticket, I had to report it to my probation officer. If I violated any of the numerous conditions or committed any crime, then I forfeited my probation. All those specific behavioral conditions were precepts.

Just as I had conditions that made up the boundaries of my probation with the state, God has rules that any who are his children must obey. In other words, they are not up for discussion. They are not optional.

We are to keep God's precepts, and that does not mean to just lock them away in a safe place so we do not lose them. It means to actively guard them; watching over, tending, preserving and observing them. These precepts, these laws, are not merely the Ten Commandments but rather the more incidental laws; all of the general responsibilities God places on us. We must enthusiastically keep even the little details of God's Word. It is not up to us to judge what is important and what is not; everything the Bible teaches us to do carries the weight of God's authoritative command, and he rightfully expects our obedience.

Rather than some radical lunatic religious nut, the psalmist here strikes me as a down-to-earth kind of person. In verses five and six he at first seems to admit his own frailty, almost sounding despairing as he cries out, "Oh, that my ways were directed and established to observe Your statutes [hearing, receiving, loving, and obeying them]! Then shall I not be put to shame [by failing to inherit Your promises] when I have respect to all Your commandments." It almost sounds as if he wants to be going only in the right direction. Clearly, he does, but there is more to this verse.

The word "steady," or "directed" in the KJV, also translates as firm or stable. In short, established.[20] When it comes to the observing or keeping the statutes of the Lord, the psalmist cries out for stability in his life. He wants to be consistent. I can sure relate to that. How about you?

Can you hear the near panic in his words? Have you ever felt this cry in your own life? Often in my walk, I have longed for steady Christian growth, and yet so many times I have chosen to follow my own map, zigzagging through life, trying on my own to get to where I wanted to be. It is important, however, to note that the verb the psalmist uses is passive. That means someone else is doing the action *to* us. This other person is holding us up so that we can stand and keep standing. If only we would all cry out with this same strong emotional and mental recognition of the need for stability in our lives, recognizing that it is God himself who holds us up and enables us to live as he has instructed us.[21]

Our godly person of Psalm 119 does not leave us wondering for long. He answers his own cry of despair with, "… when I have respect to all your commandments." You might translate that as "when I consider it all." This, of course, assumes that you look at God's commandments regularly, and not just a little of it but all of it. The verb has more to do with carefully gazing at something than simply paying attention.[22]

The apostle James tells us, "But he who looks carefully into the faultless law, the [law] of liberty, and is faithful to it and perseveres in looking into it, being not a heedless listener who forgets but an active doer [who obeys], he shall be blessed in his doing (his life of obedience)" (James 1:25).

If we are honest, then when we start looking intently at all of God's commands two things will happen: first, we feel will convicted for having violated his commands; and second, we will despair of ever being able to obey all of those commands. Yet if we follow his ways now, then one day we will look on the Word himself without shame.[23] Stick with me. This will become clearer in a minute.

Here is an example of what I mean. I used to enjoy watching the television show, "Cops." Perhaps because of what I saw on that show I sometimes feel there are just so many laws that no matter how hard I try to obey all of them, if a police officer wanted to he could probably find something wrong with me.

What is worse is when I know I have been doing something wrong like speeding. Man do I get a sick feeling when I am flying down the highway at 10 to 20 MPH over the speed limit, and suddenly see a police car in my mirror, or from the side of the road pointing a radar gun at me. I know I am both guilty and caught. There will be a price to pay.

Has your face ever burned while passing motorists looked at you while you sat in your car on the side of the road … with blue lights flashing on the police cruiser parked behind you? It is embarrassing, shameful, publicly disgracing and only the beginning. The feeling of shame or guilt is not pleasant. However, when you show regard to, or pay attention to the Lord's commandments; you will not have this feeling of shame before God.

That is why the gospel is such good news. There is a way out of that guilt and shame. When God forgives our past violations of his law, and helps us increasingly to obey it, we can look upon the law without fear of judgment for what we have done, and without fear of future failure as we face a set of standards that are humanly impossible for us to fully obey.

God deals wonderfully with both guilt and anxiety. The key is being able to hear and learn from him. A teachable, humble heart is one of the most important prerequisites. A prideful heart will only get in the way and keep you from grasping truth.

In verse seven of this psalm, the writer says, "I will praise and give thanks to You with uprightness of heart when I learn [by sanctified experiences] Your righteous judgments [Your decisions against and punishments for particular lines of thought and conduct]."

Have you ever had the experience of reading a passage of Scripture, and just being overwhelmed with how good it is to the point where you just cannot help praising God because of what you read? The more you learn about God and his Word, the more it makes you want to praise him. That is exactly what the psalmist is saying in part of this verse. Note, however, that it assumes you are doing your part by taking steps to keep learning. This is not something that just mysteriously happens to you without any apparent cause. You have to actively and regularly seek him.

Learning requires us not only to gain information but also to respond properly to it with regular action. This implies acceptance of, or submission to that information.[24] It is more than just acquiring education or accumulating knowledge: training is paramount, and quite different from knowledge.

You can see the training aspect in the term from which the word derives. It literally means an ox goad—and speaks of God using a rod (the Bible) to prod you in order to keep you on the right course. You will never reach a plateau where you will not need to learn any more from Scripture, not even if you have a doctorate in theology.

I can almost hear the exasperation in Jesus' words when the Jewish priest Nicodemus came to him.[25] Nicodemus was highly educated. As a Pharisee, he was one of the few at the pinnacle of Jewish society, and yet he was having a hard time understanding what Jesus was saying to him about being born again. He had the information, but he was not responding to it properly.

My training through the chiseling God has done in my trials is far more valuable than any degrees I may have earned. I have said for years that knowledge is meaningless unless you can *apply* what you have learned to your life in practical ways. I would much rather be wise than to possess mere knowledge. Knowledge is nothing more than accumulating information. Wisdom knows not only know how to apply knowledge but also follows through with appropriate action.

That said, the psalmist ends this part of his song with both a commitment and a plea. In verse eight, he begins with "I will keep your statutes." We might paraphrase that as "I'm going to do what you tell me to do." That is a bold statement. He is not saying to God, "I understand that what I'm doing is wrong, but just let me keep it up until I get tired of it and then I'll come around." He is saying, "I am throwing off everything that keeps me from following you. If I mess up, if I trip or fall, please do not give up on me. As much as is within me right now, I am choosing to walk with you, to obey you."

The resolve of the heart that worships God is sure: "I am going to do what you tell me to do." This is not arrogance. There is no smug self-righteousness there. Because he feels his own inadequacy for such things, he trembles at the thought of being cut adrift in the sea of uncertainty to sin.[26]

Writing of this verse, Albert Barnes said, "… he could confidently say that he would do it—yet coupled with the prayer which follows, that God would not forsake him." [27] This confidence to make such a promise to keep God's statutes is based upon the prayer that God will not leave him. His cry in the second half of this verse is, "O forsake me not utterly." We might say, "Don't walk off and leave me. Don't leave me alone to try to do this by on my own strength."

There is also a parallel to this in verse ten, where he says "Oh, let me not wander or step aside [either in ignorance or willfully] from Your commandments." God, please don't let me miss your road signs. Don't let me get off track and lost.

We may know God will never leave us or forsake us.[28] We may even believe it, but we must also realize we are powerless without him. Understand this: without God's power in our lives, we cannot keep his statutes. We simply do not have what it takes to do so. Thank God that he is not only willing but also desires to help and enable us to live the ways he calls us to live.

Enjoying God's unrestricted blessing in life comes from spending regular time in his Word; heeding his commandments, statutes, and precepts; having an understanding and teachable heart—a heart that is totally submissive to the Lord and able to discern his truths without our own biases. The mature or complete believer combines an appreciation of the Word with a dependence on the Lord, and the reward is a happy and blessed life.

Here is what so much of what ails us comes down to: we have a hard time dealing with the reality, the truth, that God does a perfect job at handling life, and he does so better than we ever can. More often than not, the fact that we have a hard time relinquishing control to God is because we do not have his Word in us and working in our lives moment to moment, day in and day out.

We can be such thickheaded people, clambering and striving to make it on our own, foolishly demanding that God go along with our plans instead of seeking his will first in all things. The plain truth is that we desperately need God in our lives, yet we pretend we can do this thing called life by our own strength of will. If we will be honest with ourselves, even we Christians have a mindset that claims there is this sacred part of life that God takes care of, and a secular or earthly part that we can handle on our own.

We have dependencies that we are unwilling to admit. First, each of us needs to come to the realization that we are dependent upon God even for the very breath we take, for every moment we live. The apostle Paul told the Athenian philosophers the same thing when he said, "For in him we live and move and have our being..."[29] Second, we must realize that we are dependent on God for insight into his Word. Third, we are dependent for guidance through life. The psalmist tells us, "Your word is a lamp to my feet and a light to my path" (Psalm 119:105).

Even though we may nod our heads in agreement, most of us rarely place all of our need for guidance in God's Word. We prefer, like the stereotypical male driver, to try to find our way on our own, and it doesn't work. It cannot work. There used to be a popular bumper sticker that said, "God is my co-pilot." Well, if God is your co-pilot you need to switch seats!

By now you may be saying to yourself, "That is all well and good, but what does any of this have to do with being chiseled by trials?" Here it comes. In 1979 when I ran my first marathon, I trained for it for a full year. I educated myself about long-distance running by reading books and articles from other long-distance runners, but if I didn't go out and put that knowledge to use then I sure was not going to be able to run 26 miles! There were days when I was tired or sore or just did not feel like running. I went out anyway... five miles, ten miles, twenty miles. There were days when I came back with muscles that screamed in pain from the lactic acid buildup in them. One day, while out on a twenty-mile run, I dehydrated and still had ten miles to go to get home. I wanted to die.

Those were certainly days of self-imposed physical trials, but because I was committed and applied the knowledge daily, I experienced the reality of long-distance running. I became trained rather than merely educated. I was a participant instead of a spectator. The difference between being knowledgeable and trained is huge for the very reason that training requires commitment and regular action. The same is true for our walk with God. We must commit our lives and walk it out daily.

Know this, when you are in the middle of life's trials, you are never alone. God does not abandon you. He is right there with you, and you can know his love and empathy if you will quiet your heart and mind and listen for his voice. He is not insensitive. He is not some white-bearded old man up in the sky with a big hammer just waiting for us to make a mistake so he can punish us again.

The writer of the book of Hebrews makes a startling statement about Jesus—one that shows how different he is from all the gods of man. He says, "For we do not have a High Priest Who is unable to understand and sympathize and have a shared feeling with our weaknesses and infirmities and liability to the assaults of temptation, but One Who has been tempted in every respect as we are, yet without sinning" (Hebrews 4:15). In other words, he is not above caring for us. He is never cold and unfeeling. He has been right where you are, he knows exactly how it feels and precisely what *you* need.

Even though he is God the Son who sits on a throne in heaven today, he gives us his empathy. He knows how we feel in these places because he has himself experienced them in the flesh. He is not a god who cannot sympathize with our physical and moral weaknesses. Quite the contrary, he understands more acutely than we ever can all the kinds of trials we go through in life.

In fact, it is precisely because he experienced all the pain and suffering through which we go—suffering injustice, experiencing the deaths of those whom he loves and of himself as well, being poor, being rejected and despised by others, enduring physical pain, and even the lingering agony of an extremely cruel death—that he is qualified to understand our sufferings. This is a God to whom we can turn when we hurt. This is a God who is there both with and for us.

If we will listen, God will answer the searing questions that invariably arise when we go through life's trials. Few of us, however, learn to hear God's voice—especially in those places—and far too few come to see how he uses the trials and tests of our lives to mold and shape us. I have been through places where I could barely crawl, much less walk. I did not relish any of them. However, it was in those very places—conversing with God about my fears, hurts and failures—that I learned to hear God's whispers of love, hope and even correction. It is because of God's hammer and chisel that I stand rooted today as a man of God. You can too.

I pray that you will not only learn to hear his voice in your hard places, but that you will come to know the depths of his love and compassion for you because you will have accepted and even embraced his hammer and chisel as he sculpts you into the man or woman of God he designed you to be.

Chiseled by Trial

POURED OUT WINE

The place where God calls you
is the place where your deep gladness
and the world's deep hunger meet.

Frederick Buechner

Today I attended the funeral of a boy I knew who was only a few weeks away from turning two when he ran into the street right in front of a truck. He died a few hours later at the hospital. It was just one of those freak accidents that drives you to your knees. For me the big question, especially when everything seems to be going wrong has always been, "Why, God? Why are you allowing this to happen to me," or "Why did you let that happen?"

It doesn't matter how spiritual you may think you are. When the difficult places of life become unbearable—when you lose your job, when your child dies, when your spouse leaves you, when you are unjustly accused, when someone you love goes off to war and comes home in a body bag, when you work hard year after year but just cannot seem to ever get caught up on the bills, when everything you have poured your life into is ripped away in an instant, when life just seems to keep on dumping all of its garbage on you—you will ask the question, "Why, God? Why me?"

Trust me, you will. This chapter is about moving from our first and natural response to suffering in which we ask why, to the better question, for what purpose, to what end?

After many pained and grief-filled experiences of my own—the deaths of my parents, the suicide attempts and eventual murder of one of my sisters, constant financial problems followed by bankruptcy, a seemingly endless stream of layoffs, repeated and serious marital problems, being arrested on felony charges over nothing more than a minor traffic accident, a child who naïvely overdosed on drugs and later struggled with anorexia, having to stick a needle into another child every night just so she would grow; seeing supposedly Christian men and women emotionally and spiritually wounding, maiming and killing the very people who most needed them; and dealing with ministers who couldn't behave properly around my wife and daughters—I was not only asking why, I was out in my front yard literally shaking my fist at the sky and screaming it out. "WHY, GOD? Why are you allowing all of this to happen to me? What do you want? You want it all? Go ahead and take it! Take my family. Take my home. Just go ahead and take everything. Take my life, please, and put me out of this misery. Go ahead. Just do it!"

Then he spoke to my heart in such a way that only he could. At the end of my rope, only God could reply in a way that would satisfy the demanding questions— questions I had good reasons to ask—and when it sank in, it left me in a shoulder heaving, sobbing heap on the sidewalk. What I heard was something we can only understand with our heart. It is spiritual, and brought to light in the heart by the Holy Spirit. He said seven life-changing words I shall never forget, *"Those whom I love most I crush."*

My immediate response was, "Whoa! What did you just say, and what in the world does *that* mean?" What God was saying to me was that the difficult places I have gone through, and will continue to go through in this life, serve two purposes: first, to reassure me of his love; and second, to crush me so I come to the place where my relationship with him is intoxicating to him, where I become set apart for his glory.

God's blessings do not come with any regularity to the rebellious, the hardheaded, or the hard-hearted. To hear his voice clearly and frequently you must first allow God to crush you, allow him to chisel away more of you so that he can then pour his wisdom into you.[1]

At first, that doesn't sit well with most of us. We like the idea of being loved by God, but what's with that part about being *crushed*? We are fine with thoughts and discussions of a loving God, but even if it *is* in our best interest we sure don't like the thought that this same loving God allows us to go through the wringer.

We have become jaded in our outlook about what God has the right to expect from us. Much to our discredit, we are quite uncomfortable with anything that smacks of right or wrong, black or white, good or bad, holy or evil. In our twenty-first century minds everything is relative. In our way of thinking, outside of us there is no supreme authority. We have fallen into the trap where what we consider right or wrong depends upon the situation, not on what God has to say. As Randal Working said, "Not even God, our culture claims, has the right to make absolutes."[2] To put it bluntly, we behave like spoiled children.

A clear-cut example of this is my own behavior. Even as a minister I all too often try to usurp God's authority. Why else was I out in my yard screaming at him? It was because he wasn't doing things the way I thought he should. I was still trying to be in charge. How foolish!

If we will be honest with ourselves, then we will admit that most of us, most of the time—even if we want to be close to God—expect such a relationship to be on our terms rather than his. I agree with Randall's summation that from a spiritual perspective we are, "naturally at odds with our Creator, our hearts and minds are clouded and we're incapable of knowing God."[3]

While we all have natural abilities, and while it is proper for us to use those God-given abilities in our various callings, it is not proper to rely on them as our source of worth or purpose. If we get caught up in our own abilities, then we have once again fallen into the trap of self-sufficiency, which is nothing more than idolism. We should instead look to God and ask ourselves, "What's next? In the long run, what does this mean?" In other words, our focus ought not to be on this particular day, week, month, year or even this present life. Instead, we should focus on eternity. Doing so will help us to better accept the sufferings of this life when appropriate, and to rely on God instead of ourselves.

The good news is that God wants to be close to us and us to him, and he is willing to do whatever it takes to win us over—including having sent his son to die in our place, in allowing us to go through the difficult places that will bring us to the point of intimately knowing him. The beginning of the road to a right relationship with God is the point where we humbly admit our need, where our cry is "God, I want more of you in my life and less of me. Chisel away."

Being crushed or chiseled is not something to which any of us looks forward. We naturally try to avoid such experiences. Let's be real here. It hurts. It is, therefore, important that I explain what I mean when I speak of being crushed. It is only when I am crushed that I can become a drink offering to God. Okay, that may be a bit confusing. I can almost hear you asking, "What in the world does *that* mean?" It is vital to grasp the significance of the drink offering, so I hope I don't lose you here. Understanding this is key to understanding what it means to be chiseled by trial.

In ancient Israel, before an altar could be used in worship, an offering—usually of wine, sometimes of oil— was poured out upon it. This act consecrated the altar to the worship and service of God. This act associated the altar with the sacred. It set it apart from common items, and made it holy.

There are two important words there. The first is the word "service," which we often find translated in our Bibles as "ministry." Ministry is simply service, not to self but to God and others. When you hear the word "ministry," think "service,"[4] for in truth that is ministry. It is not the work of a select few. It is the service of *all* Christians. The second word is "holy" which means "set apart."[5] At home we set the good silverware apart from the stainless or flatware. In contrast to everyday plates and bowls, we keep the "good china" in a separate special cabinet. Things that are holy have been set apart from common things.

If you are to be holy, then you must be set apart, but for what? The answer is simple: for service to God. Many of us incorrectly think we are here for ourselves. We are not. "Looking out for number one" is one of the biggest lies of all time. The apostle Paul put it well when he said our bodies are now God's temples, that we do not even own ourselves.[6] So to be set apart for service to God we must first be crushed in order to become drink offerings. Stick with me.

Moses wrote down all the legalities, in painstaking detail, of what was and was not to be done in worship, including the drink offering. The pitcher used for the drink offering was made of pure gold. The wine being offered was placed in the golden pitcher, and while the sacrificial lamb was burned upon the altar, the priest poured the *entire* drink offering—all three pints of strong wine—out on the ground. The drink offering was not to be consumed by the priest, but instead offered to the Lord as an aroma, a sweet smell. It belonged only to God. That is such a beautiful picture of the coming Savior, Jesus, and of the sacrifice we are called to make to him of ourselves.

God, as Christ, was not only the sacrifice, but he also made it possible for us to become a sacrifice that pleases him as well. Speaking of the sacrificial Lamb to come (Jesus), the prophet Isaiah said that he poured out his life even to the point of death.[7] Just as in all things he did, Christ was our supreme example, and particularly in this case, of becoming a drink offering to God. Just as the high priest poured out the drink offering, Jesus poured himself out to God, and so must we.

In churches across the world Christians speak of sanctification (a buzzword of sorts for becoming a drink offering) almost as some super-spiritual, pie-in-the-sky, ultimate end which only the "worthy" achieve. More often, people think of it as a behavior rather than what it is—a state of being. Well, that's religion for you, but it certainly isn't what Jesus taught. The word "sanctify" literally means, "to make holy."[8] What is sanctified has been purified, or hallowed. It is set apart for a special use or purpose—in this case, set apart for God's good pleasure.

From a theological perspective, it is the *process* of being set apart, of being made holy. Most Bible scholars agree that sanctification is a life-long process. Where differences generally occur among them is the answer to the question of at what point the process is complete. Can we reach a point of complete sanctification in this life, or will that happen when we reach heaven? I have no intention of trying to provide a conclusive answer for all people. Let the legalists argue over it until Jesus returns. What I want is to know God more closely today than yesterday, and to continue growing closer to him more and more every day.

That means becoming more like him, allowing him to chip away at me, sculpting me into the man he desires, getting to that point I discussed in the chapter on faith, where God sees his reflection in me.

While much has been written and debated over the centuries about the significances of the various offerings, that is not the purpose of this chapter. The point here is that the drink offering was an expression of the joy God takes in the completed work of Jesus; whose death by crucifixion and coming back to life bought us back, redeemed us, and set us apart (sanctified us) for God.

Just as he was not satisfied merely with bringing the Israelites out of their bondage in Egypt, God is only satisfied with us when we are complete and possess the fullness of his blessing—which is, of course, being in right relationship with him. We see this even in the story of creation. The book of Genesis tells us that when God had completed his work of creation, and while Adam and Eve were in Eden, God blessed it, set it apart, and rested from his work.[9] His work of creation was complete, and he was pleased with *all* of it. The Bible tells us that when he was finished with his work, he proclaimed it "good."

We also see this beautiful picture of the drink offering in the Old Testament where Moses wrote of the sacrificial lamb, saying that, like the drink offering, it would be a soothing aroma to God.[10] If only we could truly grasp the full significance of this: when he has brought us to the point where we are willing to be crushed, to put our selfishness aside, then the God of the universe inhales our sacrifice, and the smell of it is sweet to him. He takes great pleasure in it; we become intoxicating to him, a true drink offering.

In recent years very little has been taught concerning its significance, but I believe the drink offering is not just some odd theological idea of interest to only a few old stuffed shirts. It has a direct connection with the times in which we live. It is of paramount importance that we understand what God is saying to us about the drink offering in a day where self is king, where we seek to please and pamper ourselves; where we spend so much time, energy and money indulging our own desires.

God is calling us to pour out our very lives as a sacrifice—as drink offerings—to him. It is an invitation to empty ourselves, to pour our lives out as living sacrifices, to quit squandering all the goodness of God on our selfish wants. In other words, he is calling us to change our ways. This is how we deny ourselves and take up our cross.[11]

The Old Testament offerings and sacrifices of the Israelites didn't please God because they were nothing more than heartless ritual, lip service.[12] Jesus truly brought joy and pleasure to the Father when he poured out his life as a drink offering. This was not just a foreshadowing—an indication or picture of what is to come—it was, and is, the very substance of what God has always wanted: obedience and sacrifice from a heart in love with him.

He longs for those who, from their hearts, will do his will in *all* things. The apostle Paul said the same thing, that God doesn't delight in burnt offerings, but that he (Paul) was there to do God's will instead of his own.[13] Jesus established the pattern for all of us—showing us himself as a life poured out in service to God, doing only what God desired. It is an active and poignant way of saying, "*All* of me belongs to you, God. I'm not holding anything back. I am pouring my life out as a sacrifice to you."

This is not limited to just the Old Testament. It is equally applicable in the New. Writing to the Christians in Philippi, Paul said he poured himself out as a sacrifice and was glad to do so. He encouraged them do to likewise.[14] At the end of his ministry, just prior to his death, he was able to honestly say he was about to be poured out as a drink offering, that he had fought the good fight, and held onto his faith.[15] This apostle of self-denial stood before his Lord in the final days of his ministry as an empty pitcher, having completely emptied himself as a living sacrifice. What a shining example!

When he wrote of having fought the good fight and of having kept the faith, he was in effect saying, "I have consistently yielded my will to God's. I have poured all of me out to my Lord. I haven't held back." He gave up the world and all of its meaningless trappings, considering it all (as he put it) as so much garbage, so that he could set his affections—his desires, his priorities, his treasures—on things above, on the things of God.[16]

Am I saying God wants you to be a drink offering? Absolutely. He longs and even aches for us to pour ourselves out to him, to give up struggling and trying to be in control. Even though God has made the provision for us to be restored to him, even though we have established that he desires relationship with us, there is another side to this drink offering coin.

We find the word translated in our Bibles as "drink offering" comes from the Hebrew word which also means "molten image"—precious metals melted down to either plate a carved (graven) image, or to itself be cast as an object of worship.[17] Now, the second of the Ten Commandments tells us that we are not supposed to make any image to worship in place of him,[18] and yet throughout the ages we have quite literally melted down gold and silver to make our own gods. Figuratively, we have made gods both of things and of self.

We also find the phrase "drink offering," or "molten image," in the words of the prophet, Jeremiah, who wrote, "Every man has become like a brute, irrational and stupid, without knowledge [of God]; every goldsmith is brought to shame by his graven idols; for his molten images are frauds and falsehood, and there is no breath in them" (Jeremiah 10:14). You could paraphrase part of that as, "for his molten image—his drink offering—is a fake."

Noted bible commentator, John Gill, said of this passage's use of the phrase "molten image," "for his molten image is falsehood; it is a lie, when it is said to be a god; and it deceives those who worship it, and place any confidence in it." The psalmist affirms this, saying that their idols were lifeless, unable to speak, see, hear, smell, touch or walk.[19] I say he went on to proclaim that those who made or worshipped idols were about as smart as a box of rocks.

We fancy ourselves more sophisticated than the ancients. We think we are more cultured and wiser, and in many ways we are. And yet from birth we still make ourselves out to be gods. We make of ourselves molten images, phony drink offerings.

We will sacrifice friends and family in order to appease selfish desires. The man who abandons his wife and children in order to feed his desire for another woman (usually younger) has made himself an idol. I did, and that will haunt me the rest of my life. The mother who so dotes on her children that she refuses to let anything difficult enter their little world (that would build their character and teach them) or admit that they could ever do anything wrong, makes them her idols.

Many of us will walk over others in order to get a promotion or a raise at work. We will even recklessly endanger the lives of others just so we can get to the traffic light a few seconds before anyone else or to vainly try to prove how much better our car is than theirs, or how more important we are then are they. King Solomon said it well in Ecclesiastes, "Vapor of vapors and futility of futilities, says the Preacher. Vapor of vapors and futility of futilities! All is vanity (emptiness, falsity, and vainglory)" (Ecclesiastes 1:2).

Like it or not (and most of us don't), we are all guilty of making ourselves out to be little gods. At least even in their apparent foolishness ancient people more often worshipped something other than themselves. If we truly want to belong to God then we must reach the point where we see this truth with more than just our selfish minds.

While some of us truly desire to know God more intimately, we are dismayed that we can't get there by our own efforts. Do you see the futility of it? All our religions (including the secular humanism of so many who claim they have no religion) have thousands of rituals—none of which will get us there.

Before we can become consecrated altars, before we can be set apart as holy vessels and poured out drink offerings, we must come to the place where we see ourselves for the false gods we have set ourselves up as, and we must confess the lie. We must become true drink offerings, made so by the very hand of God.

We can no more become consecrated by our own efforts or desires than an altar can consecrate itself, or a grape can turn itself into wine. Only God can make us a drink offering, set apart for worship and service to him. Only the holy hand of God can sculpt us and crush us in order to turn us into a true drink offering.

God deeply desires to take pleasure in us. As I said previously, he is not some white-robed angry old man up in the sky just waiting for us to make a mistake so he can bring the hammer down. He desires to commune with us, to drink us in like an excellent wine. In order to make wine, grapes must first be crushed. If we are to become a drink offering to God, we too must first be crushed.

We must come to the end of ourselves. We must die to being our own gods. It is only then that we can fully understand what the apostle Paul meant when he said that he had been crucified with Christ.[20] In this oft-quoted passage, he went on to say that he no longer counted appearing righteous before others as important, but that what matters most is Christ who lives in him. Paul had discovered the importance of dying to self, which is what he meant by being crucified with Christ.

Most Christians have heard that passage quoted many times, but rarely do we hear the verse immediately following, "I am not going to go back on that. Is it not clear to you that to go back to that old rule-keeping, peer-pleasing religion would be an abandonment of everything personal and free in my relationship with God? I refuse to do that, to repudiate God's grace. If a living relationship with God could come by rule-keeping, then Christ died unnecessarily" (Galatians 2:21).

In other words, if our own efforts were enough to save us, then Christ never would have had to come as man and God to die so horribly on a cross. If, based on our own abilities, we could become worthy of an intimate relationship with God, then the crucifixion of Jesus would have been without any meaning, any value, any hope, any love.

Despite what we may say to others, none of us desires the unpleasant experiences that drive us to the cross and the end of self. However, if we are to become an intoxicating pleasure to God, then we must go through the wine press. When God crushes us it hurts. Who wants that kind of pain? Not me. And yet, however crazy it sounds, once we have been crushed and made into his wine, we will be glad of it. In our hearts we will discover that there is not any place or anything else that can satisfy our deepest longings. The pain of life's trials is not worthy of comparison with the richness of knowing God intimately.

I do not desire the "former days" before the pain of being crushed and chiseled by trial. I have no desire to go through the heartaches of death, broken trusts, betrayal, illnesses, and the myriad other problems we face in life. Even as I was revising this book my oldest sister—the last of three—died. These painful places pale compared to intimacy with God.

There was a time when I was under intense emotional pressure. My marriage was falling apart, and it seemed that my heart was being ripped out. The pain was indescribable. I had an option: turn away from God in pain, bitterness and anger, or run to him. I thank God that he led me in the right direction.

King Solomon wrote that if we recognize and acknowledge God in all our ways of life that he will direct our paths.[21] Those paths are comprised of all the steps of our lives, all the decisions and actions we take. How true, and how God has proved himself to me by keeping that promise. That was the beginning of my drawing close to God, of learning to hear his whispers of love, and of accepting his hammer and chisel.

A few years ago my youngest son, home from military duty, asked me what was my greatest fear. Without a moment's hesitation, and with tears in my eyes, I responded, "Losing the intimacy I have come to know with God."

Jesus said that we would have difficulties, trials, distress and frustrations in our lives. He also said to take courage, to be confident, to be undaunted by them.[22] Most of us can grasp the face value of that, but let's dig a little bit deeper. The phrase "difficulties" ("tribulation" in the King James Version) is the ancient Greek word for "pressure."[23] What turns grapes into wine? The answer, of course, is pressure. (Just as a point of interest, the place where Jesus faced his most difficult time—as he prayed in the Garden of Gethsemane while Judas was betraying him—means "oil press."[24])

Famed Bible commentator Matthew Henry said, "It has been the lot of Christ's disciples to have more or less tribulation in this world. Men persecute them because they are so good, and God corrects them because they are no better. Men design to cut them off from the earth, and God designs by affliction to make them meet for heaven; and so between both they shall have tribulation."[25] If you are a follower of Jesus, you must expect to have trials and tribulations in this life. If Christ had to face them, what makes any of us feel exempt?

When God crushes you, don't despair. Instead, rejoice. Embrace it. Take it as the sign of his love for you. There is no other way to intensely know God without first being crushed, made into a drink offering; crucified with Christ, your life poured out before him. Only then can you be set apart to serve God, to be used as he desires. If you hang onto yourself, you won't make it. This is partially what Jesus was talking about when he said we have to lose our life to gain it. Give up trying to be in control of your life, and instead let God be in control. He will not settle for anything less.

Why must we face trials in life? We must face them because God loves us. No trial is pleasant in its passage, but the result of each trial is that God shapes us a little more like the image of him we are supposed to be. We become better suited with each hardship to minister both to him and to those around us who also hurt. The trick, I think, is in getting our minds off of ourselves and onto those around us whom we can serve as well as onto God who loves us all so deeply.

The whole of the matter is whether or not you will come to the end of your rope. Will you discover that you cannot make it on your own, that you need a Savior? Will you learn to let go of *your* dreams, *your* desires and *your* self-centered lifestyle? God wants *all* of you, not just part. Your flesh may cry out that what God asks is unreasonable, but true fulfillment in life comes in submitting to God in all ways rather than rebelling against him.

When it comes to our Christian walk, one of the biggest fears we all have is that God is going to ask us to give up something we enjoy; or worse—gasp!—to do something we don't enjoy. So we hold back from giving him our all. So what?

What do you think would happen if you went on a job interview and told the prospective employer that you only want to show up at work, but that you don't expect actually to do anything? Or, what if you told him that you only want to work during the mornings and then take the rest of the day off? How do you think that manager would react? I don't think he'd be inclined to hire you, and you certainly wouldn't get the rewards that go with it.

Our jobs are nearly always team efforts, and when we are part of such a team, the other members have every right to expect us to do our best on the job, and regularly to put in a full day's work.

For selfish reasons many of us don't think the same applies to our relationship with God. By our attitudes and actions many of us tell him two things. First, we say that we really don't want to share in the depth of a real relationship with him. We are not willing to, day-in and day-out, be committed to the relationship. Second, we are saying we don't want to contribute anything when others may be in most need of what we can do for them.

God doesn't want just Sunday mornings from you. He wants your *whole* life, and it is only when you fully surrender it to him that he can make something extraordinary out of it. Jesus tells us, "The thief comes only in order to steal and kill and destroy. I came that they may have and enjoy life, and have it in abundance (to the full, till it overflows)" (John 10:10 AMP). If you are one of those who have held out on God, then you have yet to reach that level of trust in him. We were not meant to live our lives halfway.

You may think you can live with one foot in the world and one with God, but the truth is that you can't. Either you're sold out to God or you're sold out to the world. Jesus warned us that we can't serve two masters.[26]

In order to have that abundant life, you have to first give your full life to God. That means you don't hold back. Jesus said, "Whoever finds his [lower] life will lose it [the higher life], and whoever loses his [lower] life on My account will find it [the higher life]" (Matthew 10:39 AMP). In other words, if you cling to your life, you'll lose it; but if you give it all up to God, you save it!

If God calls you to do something you don't particularly think you want to do—say, become a missionary in a far away country without running water or basic sanitation—he still knows you better than anyone else does, including you! He made you. He knows what it will take to make you happiest. He knows what will fulfill you best, even to the point of overflowing. If you choose any other direction, then you are settling for second best (or worse).

God is not out to make your life miserable. He wants to lead each of us in the direction that will cause us to say, "That wasn't easy for me, God, but thank you for believing in me enough to put me in that place. I really had fun despite the hardship!"

Are you willing to be crushed in order to become a poured out drink offering to God? Are you willing to finally come to the end of yourself—to the place where there are no more games, no more empty explanations, no more excuses? Are you willing to admit to yourself—and to God—that you have tried to be your own god? If so, confess that to him. Allow him to crush you. He will hold you to your word, and you will need to die to your own ways and desires every day.

Chiseled by Trial

It is not a one-time event. It is a way of life. My hope and prayer is that you will come to this place of deep intimacy with God—crushed, emptied of selfish desires, turned into poured out wine, set apart for his good pleasure, chiseled, sculpted, and pressed by the very hand of the Creator. It is the best of all places in this life and in the life to come.

SUMMARY

The path of sorrow, and that path alone
Leads to the lands where sorrow is unknown.

William Cowper[1]

This book is all about how God uses the trials, difficulties and crisis of our lives to sculpt us into the men and women he desires us to be. It is also about the need to die to self and instead live for God. I have given you examples of some of the trials I have gone through. Yours may be lesser or greater. The point here is that we all have hard places through which we must go.

The key to all of this is that our grief, our pain, our suffering, our trials, are meant to draw us closer to God by giving us the patient endurance we need in life. That can be quite difficult or even impossible to accept and believe when you are in the middle of a crisis. I want you to know that there is a way. There is hope.

The disciple James said to "consider it pure joy ... whenever you face trials of many kinds..."[2] Let me tell you, that is just not going to happen if you don't know your Bible and if you're not convinced that what God says there is true. You may be able to quote scripture well, but if you don't believe it is true, then it won't help you when your life is turned upside down.

On the other hand, when you know God's Word, believe it, and have relational knowledge of him, then you will trust him to take care of you when trials come your way. The result is that you *can* have real joy in the middle of a crisis. It takes knowledge, belief and trust (faith) to produce that joy.

After telling us to count it all joy when we fall into all kinds of trials, James didn't just leave us hanging. Immediately following his command to "count it all joy" he told us *why* we can rejoice. He told us what God is doing when trials come our way. He said the trials and proving of our faith bring out endurance and steadfastness and patience.

Do you remember my story about running a marathon so many years ago? That took patient endurance. I did not run the 26+ miles grumbling and fighting all the way. I ran even when it was hard and I was in pain. I ran the full distance knowing that if I kept putting one foot in front of the other I would achieve the goal of finishing the race. That, my friend, is patient endurance. That is what James was talking about.

Life is hard. There are trials we must all face. Some are small and others are huge. To make matters worse we have an accuser who all the while whispers in our ears how we will never get through this problem or that crisis, how we should just give up and quit, how God doesn't care or isn't there. These are why we need James' reminder that God's hammer and chisel are good for us.

The Christian life is very much like a marathon. It is difficult and requires patient endurance. Some who start the Christian walk never finish. They've bought the story that, "If you just give your life to Jesus, then life will be wonderful and all your problems will be over." Well, life with Jesus *is* wonderful, but it is also hard. Keep in mind that while Jesus promised us full and complete lives, he also promised us a cross. I spoke about this a little in the last chapter. He told us that if we want to follow him then we have to deny ourselves and take up his cross.[3]

According to Jon Sterns, pastor of Franklin Vineyard Church, when we are in the thick of a crisis we generally go through three different kinds of prayer. The first is "get me out of this!" That was what I was doing when I was out in my front yard shaking my fist at the sky and yelling at God to take me out of this life. We want the pain to end. No surprise there.

The second prayer is when we realize that God is not getting us out of the mess, so we turn to "take it away." We say to God, "If I have to stick around, God, then the least you can do is to get rid of this problem for me." Can you identify with that?

Even though I will not fault anyone for feeling these ways (I often do too), these two prayers are self-centered. The focus is on self: get me away from the problem, or get the problem away from me. The third kind of prayer in a crisis is the one we need to get to: "Lord, take me into the middle of this crisis, and help me to find you there."

You see, my fellow traveler, the one thing that preeminently differentiates Christianity from all other religions is that God steps into the thick of it with us. We find our deliverance in the middle of our pain, hand in hand with God.

Our God is not capricious. He doesn't get angry or happy with us based on a whim. He is not an oppressive ruler. He loves us. He brings light into our lives when they are filled with darkness. He identifies with us. He stepped into our midst and became like us, complete with a flesh and blood face and a name: Jesus. He suffered in every way we can ever experience and therefore fully understands how we feel when we hurt or grieve.

He came to us because we needed guidance. He appears to us today because we need transformation. He will come again because we need hope. He is, as theologians put it, the indwelling God. He lives within us. This is the mystery of the gospel (the good news of Jesus Christ). Above all else, this is what keeps me going in trials—knowing that God is *in* me, *with* me and will bring me through it.

I will not demean the suffering anyone has gone through, is going through, or will ever endure. Suffering is suffering. It hurts. Our choice is whether or not we will rebel against it or embrace it and find God in it.

We are commanded to rejoice in our trials, and we can be encouraged in knowing that God allows the problems we face in life in order to work in us patient endurance. We have good reason to be joyful (joy is not the same thing as happiness).

None of this will do you any good unless you believe the Christian life is a difficult one. If you do not believe that, then you will not believe that there is a need for patient endurance. If you don't believe that there is a need for patient endurance, then you won't believe your trials are a blessing. If you view your trials as problems or annoyances instead of occasions for rejoicing, then you will not have joy. You will, however, still have problems.

Finally, when you sense that you are being crushed, be glad. I know that sounds illogical, but that is the way God works. When he crushes us (and it does hurt!) it is because he loves us. I don't think anyone ever reaches the most intimate of relationships with God until they are crushed. If you want to be used by God, if you want to know him as you have never known him before, allow him to crush you. Coming to the end of yourself is necessary. You have to realize that life is not about you. It *is* all about God. If you think otherwise then you are still worshipping yourself, and you can never be fulfilled and live a full and blessed life that way.

Instead of focusing on whatever your trial may be, think instead about the finish line. Think about Jesus right now making a place in heaven for you. Think about the day to come when you will never again have to deal with sin or death. Think about how one day you will no longer have to endure trials and tribulations. You may hurt now, but one day you will be where there is no more pain, no more tears, and no more death.

When I ran my first marathon I made it to the finish line *despite* great pain. For me it was worth it. Now, having learned some good life lessons, I run the marathon of the Christian life, still learning to rejoice in the middle of trials, but able to do so because I know God and have faith that he will keep his promises. You can do the same. Pray that in the middle of your trials the Holy Spirit will make heaven so real to you that you will be able to run all the way to the finish line, rejoicing even through tears, doubts, frustrations, anguish and grief. God is with you, and he will never leave you.

CHAPTER NOTES

Preface

[1] Proverbs 11:2

[2] James 1:2-3

[3] James 1:4

[4] και ανοιξας το στομα (kai anoixas to stoma), Matthew 5:2

Dealing with Death

[1] Hebrews 9:27

[2] Romans 12:15

[3] Strong's: Strong, James. <u>The Exhaustive Concordance of the Bible: Showing Every Word of the Text of the Common English Version of the Canonical Books, and Every Occurrence of Each Word in Regular Order,</u> electronic ed., Ontario: Woodside Bible Fellowship, 1996. G2178, ε φα παξ. From G1909 and G530; upon one occasion (only): – (at) once (for all).

[4] Isaiah 53:3a

[5] Hebrews 2:18

[6] <u>Hebrew Greek Key Word Study Bible. New International Version.</u> Copyright © 1996 by AMG International, Inc. Scripture take from the HOLY BIBLE, NEW

INTERNATIONAL VERSION®. NIV®. Copyright ©
1973, 1978, 1984 by International Bible Society. Used by
permission of Zondervan Publishing House. All rights
reserved.

[7] Tabula rasa is the Latin phrase meaning a scraped tablet
or a clean slate. It refers to the epistemological thesis that
individual human beings are born with no innate or built-
in mental content, in a word, "blank," and that their
entire resource of knowledge is built up gradually from
their experiences and sensory perceptions of the outside
world.

[8] Romans 12:3

[9] 1 Peter 3:9

[10] http://www.nightterrors.org/

[11] Bipolar Disorder. Wikipedia.
http://en.wikipedia.org/wiki/Bipolar_disorder,
12/22/2009

[12] Keller, Jeff. President of Attitude is Everything, Inc. For
more than 17 years, Jeff has delivered presentations on
attitude and motivation to businesses, groups and trade
associations throughout the United States and abroad.
Jeff is also the author of the highly acclaimed book,
Attitude is Everything.

[13] Alcoholism: Clinical & Experimental Research.
Alcoholism And Bad Neighborhoods: A Two-way Street.
Science Daily 29 August 2007. 29 April 2009

<http://www.sciencedaily.com-
/releases/2007/08/070827161245.htm>.

[14] Elliott, John, G. <u>A Burden Lifted</u>, Nashville, 1987

[15] John 11:35

[16] Psalm 56:8

[17] Psalm 116:15

[18] John 10:10

Substitute Teachers

[1] A phosphene is an entopic phenomenon characterized by
the experience of seeing light without light actually
entering the eye. The word phosphene comes from the
Greek word phos (light) and phainein (to show).
Mechanical, electrical, or magnetic stimulation of the
retina or visual cortex as well as random firing of cells
can directly induce phosphenes in the visual system.
People who go long periods under the influence of drugs,
especially a hallucinogen, have also reported
phosphenes. (Wikipedia, www.wokipedia.com,
http://en.wikipedia.org/wiki/Phosphene).

[2] Keillor, Garrison. <u>Lake Woebegon Days</u> (New York:
Penguin Books, 1985)

[3] Ephesians 6:12

[4] <u>Easy Rider</u>, Peter Fonda, Dennis Hopper, Terry Southern,
1969

[5] Proverbs 4:23

Suffering Injustice

[1] 2 Corinthians 11:23-28

[2] National Institute of Mental Health: "The Numbers Count: Mental Illness in America," Science on Our Minds Fact Sheet Series. Accessed August 1999. Netscape: http://www.nimh.gov/publicat/number.cfm

[3] John 16:33

[4] Hebrews 12:10

[5] Barnes, Albert. Albert Barnes' Notes on the Bible.

[6] Kendall, R. T., Total Forgiveness. Lake Mary: Charisma House, 2002

[7] Galatians 6:7b

[8] Proverbs 24:16a

[9] Romans 7:15

[10] 1 Samual 13:14

[11] John 16:33

[12] Isaiah 41:10

[13] James 1:27, Galatians 2:10, Hebrews 13:3

[14] Matthew 25:40

[15] Ibid—Isaiah 41:10

[16] Matthew 28:20b, Hebrews 13:5b

Fake It Till You Make It

[1] Proverbs 22:6

[2] Despair, Inc., Austin, TX

[3] Job 1:1

[4] "Colossians 3:22-23

[5] Strong's G1401, δοῦλος, doo'-los, a slave (literally or figuratively, involuntarily or voluntarily; frequently therefore in a qualified sense of subjection or subservience), bond (-man), servant.

[6] Colossians 1:27

Feeling Worthless

[1] Romans 7 (cf)

[2] Strong's no. H7854. שׂטן saw-tawn'. From H7853; an opponent; especially (with the article prefixed) Satan, the arch enemy of good: - adversary, Satan, withstand.

[3] Revelation 12:10

[4] 1 John 3:20-21

[5] Stott, John R. W. The Letters of John: Tyndale New Testament Commentaries. Grand Rapids: 1988 revised edition.

[6] Bond, Ian A.H., Vice-President, Beacon University

[7] 1 John 3:10

[8] Hebrews 4:16

[9] "1 John 3:19

[10] Ibid

[11] F.F. Bruce

[12] Ibid

Stinking Thinking

[1] Bovee, Christian Nevell; a Christian author and lawyer who lived in the 1800s.

[2] This phrase refers to an alcoholic's reversion to old thought patterns and attitudes. Stinking thinking may include, blaming others, alcoholic grandiosity, faultfinding, self-centeredness, and skipping meetings. Stinking thinking is a warning sign to an alcoholic that he is not working the AA program and he or she is getting precariously close to their next drink. (Taken from http://www.ipass.net/a1idpirat/AAglossary.html)

[3] Lucado, Max. Facing Your Giants, Nashville: Thomas Nelson, 2006

[4] Matthew 22:39

[5] "Proverbs 16:18

[6] Philippians 2:1-2

[7] Ephesians 4:12

[8] Strong's G1249. διάκονος (dee-ak'-on-os), "1 one who executes the commands of another, esp. of a master, a servant, attendant, minister. 1A the servant of a king. 1B a deacon, one who, by virtue of the office assigned to him by the church, cares for the poor and has charge of and distributes the money collected for their use. 1C a waiter, one who serves food and drink.

[9] Proverbs 6:16-19

[10] Romans 12:2

[11] John 16:31-33

[12] Psalm 119:71

[13] Philippians 4:12-13

[14] Proverbs 3:6-7a

[15] John 8:3-11

[16] Romans 2:11

[17] Romans 2:11

[18] Philippians 4:8

[19] 1 John 4:18

[20] Romans 12:2

[21] 2 Corinthians 5:17

[22] Romans 8:28-29

[23] Proverbs 18:21a

[24] Genesis 37-47

[25] Ibid, Romans 12:2

[26] Matthew 6:25

[27] Adam Clarke, <u>Adam Clarke's Bible Commentary</u>

Call Me Hosea

[1] Exodus 20:3

[2] "Nehemiah 9:17

[3] 1 Peter 1:18-19

[4] Matthew 6:15

[5] Isaiah 55:8

[6] Matthew 18:22

[7] Mark 10:2-5

They Kill Their Own

[1] Luke 22:24

[2] 1 Corinthians 3:3

[3] Yancey, Philip. <u>What's So Amzing About Grace?</u> Grand Rapids, Zondervan. 1997

[4] Matthew 9:12

[5] Acts 17:11

[6] Strong's G1249

[7] Ezekiel 34:1-10

[8] Luke 18:1

Ephesians 6:18

[9] Pauwels, Steve. Pastor of then Living Way Church (now Christ the King) in Londonderry, New Hampshire

[10] Galatians 6:1

Keeping the Faith

[1] Kaplan, Robert D. <u>Hog Pilots, Blue Water Grunts</u>, New York: Vintage Books, 2008

[2] Hebrews 11:6

[3] Sweig, Fred. Silversmith, Society of American Silversmiths, Providence, Rhode Island

[4] 1 Corinthians 12:7-11

[5] Genesis 37:5

[6] Judges 6:12

[7] Genesis 2-12

[8] Genesis 22

[9] 1 Samuel 13:14, Acts 13:22

[10] Chambers, Oswald. <u>My Utmost for His Highest</u>, Westwood: Barbour and Company, Inc., 1935, 1963

[11] Matthew 6:31-32

[12] Psalm 34:8a

[13] Malachi 3:10

[14] Romans 12:3

[15] Acts 3:6

[16] Hebrews 11:6

[17] C.S. Lewis (1898-1963) was a novelist, literary critic, and "lay theologian" who converted to Christianity after many years as an atheist. He set out to disprove the existence of God, but instead came not only to the point of being a theist but also of believing in Jesus Christ.

[18] Lee Strobel (1952-) was a journalist trained in law who also set out to disprove the existence of God and wound up as an apologist (one who defends the Christian faith). He has written several contemporary books about God, Christ, faith, and creation.

[19] Hebrews 11:1

[20] John 20:31

[21] 1 John 5:13

[22] Kenneth Samuel Wuest (1893-1962), a noted New Testament Greek (Κοινή) scholar, professor of New Testament Greek at the Moody Bible Institute in Chicago, and publisher of over a dozen books on the New Testament.

[23] Wuest, Kenneth S. Wuest's Word Studies from the Greek New Testament: For the English Reader, Grand Rapids: Eerdmans, 1997

[24] Dr. Spiros Zodhiates (1922-2009) was a Greek-American Bible scholar, author, and ministry innovator. He was best known for his work in developing AMG (Advancing the Ministries of the Gospel) International, a Christian missions and relief agency with operations in over 40 countries, and for publishing The Hebrew-Greek KeyWord Study Bible, which indexes key terms in the English Bible with the words they were translated from in the original languages (Wikipedia, http://en.wikipedia.org/wiki/Spiros_Zodhiates).

[25] Zodhiates, Spiros, Warren Baker, Tim Rake and David Kemp. Hebrew-Greek Key Word Study Bible, Chattanooga: AMG, 1996

[26] Cottle, Ronald E. Beatitudes The Christian's Declaration of Independence, Columbus: Christian Life Publications

[27] Working, Randall. From Rebellion to Redemption: A Journey Through the Great Themes of Christian Faith. Colorado Springs: NavPress, 2001 (The Heidelberg Catechism is a Protestant confessional document, approved in 1523 A.D., that makes use of a series of questions and answers for teaching Reformed Christian doctrine.)

[28] Romans 10:17

[29] Barnes, Albert. Albert Barnes' Notes on the Bible.

[30] 2 Peter 1:4-8

[31] Ibid—Romans 10:17

[32] Working, Randall. Ibid.

Staying In the Zone

[1] Matthew 28:19

[2] Matthew 10:44

[3] Strong's H833. אשר aw-share'. A primitive root; to be straight (used in the widest sense, especially to be level, right, happy); figuratively to go forward, be honest, prosper: - (call, be) bless (-ed, happy), go, guide, lead, relieve.

[4] Strong's H835. אשר eh'-sher. From H833; happiness; only in masculine plural construction as interjection, how happy!:–blessed, happy.

[5] Strong's H8549. תמים taw-meem'. From H8552; entire (literally, figuratively or morally); also (as noun) integrity, truth: - without blemish, complete, full, perfect, sincerely (-ity), sound, without spot, undefiled, upright (-ly), whole.

[6] Strong's H8451. תורה to-raw'. From H3384; a precept or statute, especially the Decalogue or Pentateuch: - law.

[7] Brown, Francis, S., R. Driver, & C. A. Briggs. A Hebrew and English Lexicon of the Old Testament With an Appendix Containing the Biblical Aramaic Based on the Lexicon of William Gesenius. Oak Arbor: Oxford University Press, 1978. (Hereafter referred to as BDB.) Strong's, TWOT, and GK references. p. 726.1

8 Strong's H5341. נצר naw-tsar'. A primitive root; to guard, in a good sense (to protect, maintain, obey, etc.) or a bad one (to conceal, etc.): - besieged, hidden thing, keep (-er, -ing), monument, observe, preserve (-r), subtil, watcher (-man).

9 BDB, p. 205.1

10 Harris, R. L., G. L. Archer & B. K. Waltke. Theological Wordbook of the Old Testament. Chicago: Moody Press, 2003. (Hereafter referred to as TWOT). No. 1576

11 Barnes, Albert. Albert Barnes' Notes on the Bible

12 Deuteronomy 32:4

13 1 John 3:9

14 Pixar Animation Studios, A Bug's Life, 1998 (website http://www.pixar.com)

15 Strong's H1870. דרך deh'-rek. From H1869; a road (as trodden); figuratively a course of life or mode of action, often adverbially: - along, away, because of, + by, conversation, custom, [east-] ward, journey, manner, passenger, through, toward, [high-] [path-] way [-side], whither [-soever].

16 Isaiah 30:21

17 Strong's H6680. צוה tsaw-vaw'. A primitive root; (intensively) to constitute, enjoin: - appoint, (for-) bid. (give a) charge, (give a, give in, send with) command (-er, ment), send a messenger, put, (set) in order.

[18] TWOT, no. 1802

[19] Swanson, J. Dictionary of Biblical Languages with Semantic Domains: Hebrew (Old Testament) (Electronic ed.). Oak Harbor: Logos Research Systems, Inc, 1997. No. 7218

[20] Strong's H3559. כּוּן koon. A primitive root; properly to be erect (that is, stand perpendicular);. Hence (causatively) to set up, in a great variety of applications, whether literal (establish, fix, prepare, apply), or figurative (appoint, render sure, proper or prosperous): - certain (-ty), confirm, direct, faithfulness, fashion, fasten, firm, be fitted, be fixed, frame, be meet, ordain, order, perfect, (make) preparation, prepare (self), provide, make provision, (be, make) ready, right, set (aright, fast, forth), be stable, (e-) stablish, stand, tarry, X very deed.

[21] Jeremiah 10:23

[22] Ibid

[23] 1 John 2:28; 1 John 3:2

[24] Ibid, no. 4240

[25] John 3:1-21

[26] 1 Corinthians 10:12; 2 Peter 3:17

[27] Ibid. Albert Barnes

[28] 1 Kings 8:57

[29] Acts 17:28

Poured Out wine

[1] Proverbs 11:2

[2] Working, Randall. <u>From</u> <u>Rebellion</u> <u>to</u> <u>Redemption:</u> <u>A</u> <u>Journey</u> <u>Through</u> <u>the</u> <u>Great</u> <u>Themes</u> <u>of</u> <u>Christian</u> <u>Faith,</u> Colorado Springs: NavPress, 2001

[3] Ibid, Working, Randall

[4] Zodhiates, Spiros, Warren Baker, Tim Rake and David Kemp. <u>Hebrew-Greek</u> <u>Key</u> <u>Word</u> <u>Study</u> <u>Bible,</u> Chattanooga: AMG, 1996. G1248, διακονία,diakonía; gen. diakonías, fem. noun from diákonos (G1249), deacon, servant. Service, attendance, ministry. Verb, diakonéō (G1247), to minister, serve. (I) Service towards a master or guest, at table or in hospitality

[5] Ibid. G4.

[6] 1 Corinthians 6:19

[7] Isaiah 53:12

[8] Strongs, G37. ἁγιάζω, hagiazō, hag-ee-ad'-zo From <u>G40</u>; to make holy, that is, (ceremonially) purify or consecrate; (mentally) to venerate: - hallow, be holy, sanctify.

[9] Genesis 2:2-3

[10] Numbers 28:8

[11] Matthew 16:24

[12] Hebrews 10:6

[13] "Hebrews 10:7

[14] Philippians 2:17-18

[15] 2 Timothy 4:6-7

[16] "Philippians 3:8

[17] Strongs H5262. נֶסֶךְ נֵסֶךְ, nesek nêsek, neh'-sek, nay'-sek. From H5258; a libation; also a cast idol: - cover, drink offering, molten image.

[18] Exodus 20:4

[19] Psalm 115:4-8

[20] Galatians 2:20

[21] Proverbs 3:6

[22] John 16:33

[23] Strong's G2347. θλίψις, thlipsis, thlip'-sis. From G2346; pressure (literally or figuratively): - afflicted, (-tion), anguish, burdened, persecution, tribulation, trouble.

[24] Zodhiates, Spiros, Warren Baker, Tim Rake and David Kemp. Hebrew-Greek Key Word Study Bible, Chattanooga: AMG, 1996. G1068, Γεθσημανῆ, Gethsēmanê; fem. proper noun transliterated from the Aramaic gath (H1660), a press and shemen (H8081), oil. Gethsemane, meaning oil press, a place across the Kedron and at the foot of the Mount of Olives, noted as the scene of our Lord's agony...

[25] Henry, Matthew, <u>Matthew</u> <u>Henry's</u> <u>Commentary</u> <u>on</u> <u>the</u> <u>Whole</u> <u>Bible:</u> <u>Complete</u> <u>and</u> <u>Unabridged</u> <u>in</u> <u>One</u> <u>Volume</u> (Peabody: Hendrickson, 1996, c1991). Jn 16:28.

[26] Matthew 6:24

Summary

[1] Cowper, William: English poet and hymnodist who lived in the 18th century. His writings were very popular and changed the direction of 18th century nature poetry.

[2] James 1:2-4

[3] Mark 8:324-35

Chiseled by Trial

ABOUT THE AUTHOR

Gardiner B. Jones III was born and raised in Honolulu, Hawaii. He holds a Master of Sacred Studies degree from Christian Life School of Theology. He and his wife raised four children, and now live near Nashville, Tennessee.

His desire is seeking deeper knowledge of the Lord, and sharing that knowledge with others in ways they can easily grasp and use. The lessons he teaches come out of his own many years of life's trials combined with a solid theological education. His style is clear and easy to follow. He teaches, "… line upon line, precept upon precept." His first book, "Chiseled by Trial: Sculpted by God," will grip you with its frankness and insight.

Strong in integrity and doctrinal beliefs, he has the heart of one softened by the Master.

Chiseled by Trial

CPSIA information can be obtained
at www.ICGtesting.com
Printed in the USA
LVHW020932130819
627415LV00005B/8/P

9 780578 053677